ZECHARIA SITCHIN
and the Extraterrestrial
Origins of Humanity

ZECHARIA SITCHIN
and the **Extraterrestrial**
Origins of **Humanity**

M. J. Evans, Ph.D.

Bear & Company

Rochester, Vermont • Toronto, Canada

Bear & Company
One Park Street
Rochester, Vermont 05767
www.BearandCompanyBooks.com

Bear & Company is a division of Inner Traditions International

Library of Congress Cataloging-in-Publication Data
Names: Evans, M. J. (Professor emeritus), author.
Title: Zecharia Sitchin and the extraterrestrial origins of humanity / M.J. Evans, Ph.D.
Description: Rochester, VT : Bear & Company, 2016. | Includes bibliographical references and index.
Identifiers: LCCN 2016002580 (print) | LCCN 2016010498 (e-book) | ISBN 9781591432555 (pbk.) | ISBN 9781591432562 (e-book)
Subjects: LCSH: Sitchin, Zecharia. | Civilization, Ancient—Extraterrestrial influences. | Civilization—History. | Human beings—Origin. | Extraterrestrial beings. | Human-alien encounters.
Classification: LCC CB156 .E98 2016 (print) | LCC CB156 (e-book) | DDC 930—dc23
LC record available at http://lccn.loc.gov/2016002580

Printed and bound in the United States by Versa Press, Inc.

10 9 8 7 6 5 4 3

Text design by Priscilla Baker and layout by Virginia Scott Bowman
This book was typeset in Garamond Premier Pro and Futura with Utopia used as the display typeface.

To send correspondence to the author of this book, mail a first-class letter to the author c/o Inner Traditions • Bear & Company, One Park Street, Rochester, VT 05767, and we will forward the communication.

This book is dedicated to
Aaron, whose loving support
encouraged its writing,
and who helped me
to live again,
and to
Zecharia Sitchin,
whose energetic
scholarship serves as a
beacon for all those
who search for
enlightenment.

Contents

Acknowledgments

This book draws on my professional and personal contact with Zecharia Sitchin and his works over nearly twenty years. It was mostly written during 2013–2014 from my desk in Alanya, Turkey, where the view of the majestic Taurus Mountains from my balcony provided valuable spiritual energy that energized my thoughts.

I elected to live in Turkey, a beautiful mountainous country, to continue to explore the many ancient sites that dot that country's landscapes. I was reminded that there I shared the same landmass that was walked on by the Nefilim, Anunnaki, and Sumerians, the "ancient ones" who were the focus of Sitchin's several books. The friend who reminded me of this geographic connection deserves recognition for his insight (thanks, Jim). While I know with certainty that the ancient spirits were available to help me shape this manuscript, I have no doubt that Zecharia's spirit also helped me pull his most interesting contributions together and stimulated my thoughts about how to unpack them.

Many of my Sitchin friends, those who also knew him as teacher and friend, encouraged this book. Special mention goes to Joyce Thielen, John Cogswell, Lena Jacobson, Suzi and Dennis

Strauch, Wally Motloch, Jennifer Stein, Barry Baumgarten, and Nora Gottlieb. To the spirit of Fritz Meyer (who passed as the final chapter was underway), I send prayers for a safe journey as he joins Zecharia "up there." He was one of the first Sitchin "fans" and along with his wife, Judy, was supportive of my work.

I am particularly indebted to my Turkish colleague, Suat Dokumaci, who helped me through frustrating computer glitches and answered my questions about ancient sites, Islam, and Turkish culture. His family—Mine, Rana, Azra, and Asya—took great care to provide me with a sense of family and home life during my long stay in their country.

My family in Syracuse, New York, North and South Carolina, and other farflung places across the United States provided me with the support and encouragement I needed to engage fully in my writing and travel adventures.

This work owes a debt of gratitude to the staff at Inner Traditions without whose encouragement, support, and technical assistance the book would have never "seen the light of day." Special thanks go to Jeanie Levitan, editor in chief; Jennie Marx, project editor; Nancy Yeilding, copy editor; and Jon Graham, acquisitions editor.

Zecharia Sitchin— Author, Ancient Historian, and Explorer of Archaeology

If a man does not keep pace with his companions,
perhaps it is because he hears a different drummer.
Let him step to the music which he hears,
however measured or far away.

HENRY DAVID THOREAU, *WALDEN*

Zecharia Sitchin was a dedicated researcher who undertook to unravel every unanswered challenge embedded in the materials he studied. He followed his intellectual curiosity and used it to work "outside the box" (if necessary) to pursue clues he discovered. His tendency for independent thinking surfaced when he was a child, when he made an astute observation that he believed to be a translation error in the biblical Book of Genesis. The word *Nefilim* had been translated as "giants," but he believed that translation was incorrect. When he tried to get his teacher's assistance to confirm the accuracy of his observation, he was told not to question The Bible. Thereafter, unable to abandon his belief

Fig. P.1. Zecharia Sitchin on a tour in Mexico.
(Photograph by Wally Motloch)

that the word, when accurately translated, actually means *"those who came down,"* he launched a quest to find evidence answering this question: *Who* came down? His search for the answer took him from childhood across a long journey of study and research.

Previous scholars were unable to fully interpret and accurately decipher what—in Sitchin's judgment—was the actual story of the ancient space travelers as told on the Sumerian clay tablets. The scholars who first worked on the tablets did their writing at the end of the nineteenth century and in the first decade of the twentieth century. The space age did not develop for several decades after those pioneers did their work. As a result, these early researchers and scholars had *no context* within which to understand the space age material they were reading, and their first published works showed that they thought the tablets were mythology. Sitchin, on the other hand, was conversant with modern space age technology and recognized it in the ancient records.

Because Sitchin taught himself to read Sumerian and the languages that derived from it—namely Akkadian, Babylonian, and ancient Hebrew—he had the linguistic skills that allowed him to recognize the truth embedded in the information he read. He fervently believed the tablet records were not telling of mythical beliefs of the ancient people. As new space age events emerged in modern times, he mastered cosmology, celestial mechanics, and even genetic science, which provided the explanations that matched the true meanings. In essence, with the modern science, he found the "key" to fully understand the actual meaning embedded in the ancient clay tablets.

Through his penetrating analysis, Sitchin discovered that these stories were reports *of what actually happened* when an ancient civilization came to Earth using their highly advanced capability for interplanetary travel. The information Sitchin uncovered from his own reading and translation of the cuneiform script told a fascinating story. These first settlers came in space vehicles to obtain gold needed on their planet; they used advanced space technology to transship the gold they found here back to their home planet. This is the essence of the content that Sitchin found in the tablet materials and he brought it to light for modern society's edification as his scholarly and personal contribution.

* * *

It must have been a twist of fate that prompted me to attend a conference with the unusual title, "When Cosmic Cultures Meet," an event organized by the Human Potential Foundation. On May 26, 1995 I arrived at the conference venue, the Washington

Sheraton Hotel, with only the expectation of exercising my academic curiosity by listening to informative presentations by notable researchers like John Mack, M.D., Ruth Montgomery, Richard Boyland, Ph.D., R. Leo Sprinkle, Ph.D., Charles Tart, Ph.D., and J. J. Hurtak, Ph.D., and the well-known futurist, John Peterson, to name just a few of the several presenters. My expectation was that these experts would enlarge my understanding of phenomena that represented intrusions by other galactic cultures into Earth's realm and illuminate intercultural contact between "them" and us.

My curiosity about this topic was informed by my reading about the 1947 unidentified flying object (UFO) that crashed in Arizona. In the first few days the original information about this UFO crash that left debris scattered across a large crash site made the published news media. But within a few days, following the takeover of the site and its debris by the U.S. military, the original report was contradicted. What was fascinating in the original news report was that "beings" were found on board the vehicle. The mystery about what happened to the beings and the debris continued to deepen as time passed. Was there cultural contact? That question haunts the interested public as there still are few clear answers. The original report implied the real possibility of alien contact with Earth's inhabitants, so I wanted to know more about what current researchers had to say about this possibility.

The conference presenters were selected because they held expertise derived from their studies of human reactions to alien contact. A few experts had examined individuals who had been abducted by UFOs and I was curious about what the human reactions were to "alien encounters." I intuitively believed that a very real possibility existed that Earth space was being "observed" (and perhaps "penetrated") by beings from beyond our solar system.

Little did I know that attending that conference not only would enlarge my knowledge about interspecies cultural contact, but it would reset my academic focus from Earth-based studies (I am a professional geographer) to the planets in our solar system and the galaxy beyond. Most notable was that the conference presentations stimulated my interest in a very different body of evidence than I had been exposed to throughout my academic studies and career.

The stated purpose of the conference event was to energize development of a government policy dealing with disclosure of information about the extraterrestrial (ET) and unidentified flying object (UFO) phenomena that was well underway. This possible contact seemed to be increasing, especially since the detonation of atomic bombs used to end the war in the Pacific. The organizers of this conference held a certainty that more contact with galactic civilizations would occur in the future, and they sought expert views to understand the impact of these encounters, and to illuminate evidence that would counter the secrecy stance of the government.

This conference was intended to be a capstone on a process that had been ongoing at the White House for more than two years. It was a deliberate step undertaken by the organizers to get the U.S. government to disclose its collected evidence on alien contact. Sitchin's contribution to these discussions of this conference slid a deep historical body of information under the contemporary evidence of contact with civilizations from outer space. The question this conference provoked was, "Is alien contact real?" The Sitchin answer was: "It certainly is; it happened before and will happen again."

At the time of his first talk, I had never heard of Zecharia Sitchin. He was listed to be fifteenth on the conference agenda, and his presentation was titled "The Past Holds the Key to the Future." He also was a participant later on the agenda in a three-person panel focused on the future impact of encounters with galactic cultures. What he emphasized in both talks was that cosmic cultures already have met. He pointed out that the records of the past are replete with information and evidence on the subject of contact, and he urged the audience to recognize that we humans must study the past in order to be prepared for the future. Sitchin ended his first presentation with these words:

> The realization that we are not alone, even in our own solar system, and the coming re-encounter with another, more advanced civilization, should be at the top of humanity's agenda. In that respect, a conference such as this is an important step in the right direction. . . . To know the future, study the past.[1]

This last statement proved to be a steadfast belief often voiced by Sitchin in his in-person presentations and also was emphasized in his writings. He firmly believed that the past informs what will happen in the future. In these presentations, his style was unassuming, highly informative, and very captivating.

When the Futures panel assembled on the podium, and when it was Sitchin's turn to speak, he again spoke in a clear manner, dealing first with what he believed was the obvious mistake in the conference title, "When Cosmic Cultures Meet." He offered a correction, saying that to be historically accurate, the conference title should have been stated in the past tense. Sitchin's reason to believe that cosmic contact already had taken place was based on his own research findings. He explained that the contact of "other terrestrials" (OTs)* with Earth had occurred many thousands of years ago. Space explorers' initial arrival on Earth was found to be 445,000 years ago. Sitchin's own words were captured by the conference organizers, who had all the presentations transcribed and published, and then sent to each attendee.

> About 445,000 years ago, people from another planet arrived on earth. The Sumerians called them Anunnaki, which in Sumerian, means literally, "Those who from heaven to earth came." They say they originally came for their own purposes in search of gold because they needed gold, not for jewelry, not for making coins or medallions, but they needed it for the survival of their own planet as the atmosphere, or its heat, was dissipating. The only way they could protect their planet was by creating a shield of gold particles to keep the heat and the atmosphere in. At first, they landed a group of 50 who splashed down in the Persian Gulf. They waded ashore. There is a very long [ancient] text, very detailed explaining this [event].

> By the way, all of the texts that I will mention in these few minutes and the hundreds of them that are [discussed] in my books, and none of them have been discovered by me. I do not claim anywhere that I went to one of the ancient sites, like Mesopotamia, and poked with my stick in the ground, saying

---

*This is a term I have coined because Sitchin described the planet that sent space travelers to Earth as a "terrestrial planet."

"I found a tablet and look what it says—nobody knew it before but I now discovered it." Every text and every depiction was discovered by others. They are all in well-known and prestigious museums. The text, and the pictures [supporting them] were published, republished, translated, and transliterated by others, except that through my detailed knowledge of Sumerian, Akkadian, early Hebrew, and other languages, I was able to read them and judge their accuracy for myself. They are very detailed. The only difference between me and all of the scholars who are aware of them is that all of this tablet information, all of these tablet texts, are *called mythology* [by traditional scholars].[2]

He then revealed the key he used to unlock the actual meaning in the ancient scripts. He entered the ancient tablet evidence with a mindset that saw the tablets as *historical accounts*—not myth. His research questions were fueled by these statements: "What if all this information scribed on the ancient tablets is *true,* all the stories also are true, and are not myths?* What if all the information reported on the ancient tablets really happened?"

* * *

In retrospect, the highlights of this entire conference event for me were the presentations by Zecharia Sitchin. He emphasized that his discussion was drawn from documentable evidence that fully explained the reality of prior contact. It consisted of the existence of a planet that comes into our solar system approximately every 3,600 years and brings its inhabitants within reach of planet Earth. Those space travelers—who called themselves Nefilim (the

---

*The implication here is that myths are made up stories, filled with imagination and even fantasy.

royalty of their society) and Anunnaki (the rank and file)—then came to Earth to search for gold, and originally settled Earth in order to carry out that mission. Gold was need on their home planet to prevent erosion of their atmosphere.

Well before this conference, I had traveled across Ireland and Great Britain to intensify my long-standing interest in discovering who built the enigmatic megastone structures (like dolmen and ancient stone circles) and why they were built thousands of years ago in the locations where we find them today. I was convinced, even before I learned of Sitchin's findings, that the promulgated explanations of the purposes of these structures were incomplete.

I had studied the legend of "The Battle of Moytura," telling of the Tuatha de Dann of ancient Ireland. They were a race of people who are thought to have originated in the northern mountains of the world, and held advanced "magical" skills and knowledge. The Tuatha de came south, landed, burned their ships to eliminate the idea of escape, and were considered "invaders" by the indigenous tribes. Eventually three wars were carried out with these original inhabitants. Those indigenous folk (the Fir Bolg and Fomoire) viewed this race of newcomers in different ways. They were not considered gods. Their "magic" might have been the skills and knowledge of the space travelers Sitchin spoke about.

When I asked Sitchin if these "invaders" were Anunnaki, he sidestepped my question and asked if I had read any of his books. Apparently there was more for me to learn from his work that would help me answer my question for myself. I went home and over the next few months read his six books that were then in print.

After my first Sitchin encounter, I traveled again to Britain and Ireland. My travels that summer took me to the most well-known ancient megastone site in Britain—Stonehenge. I marveled

Fig. P.2. Stonehenge, in southern England.

at the size of the stones used to form the ancient circles. I was amazed to learn how far away the quarry sites for some of the stones were from the finished structures. I also visited and studied the megastones that comprised the 2600 B.C. site of Avebury, and dolmen structures in Ireland. These monuments presented evidence of ancient people's beliefs that are different from those of today's population. Who were these people who built these stone monuments? Why did they select the landscapes on which they are found today?* Zecharia Sitchin opened a completely new vista for me. I came away from those revisited sites in England and Ireland with new perspectives and a very different set of ques-

---

*It is obvious that today's landscapes differ significantly from those of ancient times, but distances to water courses and oceans as well as mountains basically are the same.

Fig. P.3. One of the Avebury stones.
Author is shown seated in the "Devil's Chair."

tions to explore. It became clear to me that a new hypothesis was forming in my mind. Was it possible the space travelers of whom Sitchin wrote, built many—if not most—of the huge megastone structures I had seen on the British and Irish landscapes?

After exposure to the information in Sitchin's books, I elected to join an upcoming tour Sitchin organized to explore ancient Mediterranean sites where possible evidence of the Anunnaki presence still could be seen. The evidence he showed his interested travel groups was not only fascinating, but it appeared to reveal evidence of megastone structures that unquestionably were beyond human capabilities to construct.

One important aspect of my participation in that Sitchin tour gave me a unique research opportunity. In the course of these travels, I interviewed the participants that Sitchin called

*Fig. P.4. Sitchin responds to questions
from the author and a fellow traveler.*

his "fans." I wanted to discover who these individuals were, and how they came to appreciate—and accept—Sitchin's findings* I found them to be curious people from various backgrounds in such fields as engineering, law, business, and applied science; they were airline employees and pilots, computer experts, former travel agents and technicians. Also in these groups were curious people who had read Sitchin's books and wanted to know more about him and his findings. They all were thoughtful, very intelligent, keenly inquisitive people, and knew how to separate "garbage from good stuff." On the whole, these travelers were intellectually adept people who were not easily "hoodwinked"; they were independent thinkers, accustomed to evaluating information. They found validity in Sitchin's work that was reassuring to my (then) academically based skepticism.

---

*Sitchin referred to those who accepted his work as his "fans."

Fig. P.5. Sitchin with a group of fans in the field.

Taken together, Sitchin's fans were inquiring individuals who accepted his well-researched information, judging it to be well documented and well reasoned. They also stayed loyal to the validity of his work in spite of what turned out to be a wave of negative reactions from a stratum of the intellectual establishment. That negativity was aired on the Internet: it appeared not only in the form of criticism of Sitchin's findings, but took the form of attacks on the logic that informed his interpretations. These criticisms even went so far as to impugn the fact that he was putting forth academically based research findings and did not hold a faculty position or Ph.D.* The implication of such criticisms suggested—without direct accusation—that a nonacademic was publishing research based

---

*It must be mentioned that Sitchin came from an academic family, and his own graduate degree from the London School of Economics provided him with a "proper" knowledge of academic traditions.

in the scientific and archaeological realm, something even a knowledgeable layperson was not qualified to do. Some labeled his findings "pseudoscience." Obviously academic elitism was at work in their articulated criticism—implying that only those with advanced academic training would be qualified to work with complex material, and only those with that type of background would be able to reason in sophisticated, academically valid ways.

The criticisms of Sitchin's work prompted me to look into how new bodies of explanation enter the scholarly arena, and what happens to those who are bold enough to amass information that has no existing literature to serve as a platform. As one schooled in academic literature, I could see no difference in the quality of Sitchin's work as compared with the hundreds of volumes of academic material—both theoretical and applied—that I studied in the pursuit of my own advanced degrees and teaching work in academia.

I came to realize that Sitchin's work held the promise of actually shifting the existing explanatory paradigm of Earth's history of settlement, and also builds a new platform for understanding the history of the human species. Dealing with information that clearly *enlarges* the way we think of causation and explanation is not new in the history of science, but examples of new ways of thinking are uncommon. To enlarge the way explanatory models in the study of the history of science are dealt with, the experts refer to the new perspectives and explanatory frameworks as a *new paradigm*. Completely new ways of explanation shift the meaning of many well-studied phenomena, making some concepts irrelevant and opening up new frontiers for exploration. A scholar who sets out new explanations has a "rocky road" to travel.* On these rare occasions when new explanations emerge, if this new evidence is sufficiently powerful enough to *shift the explanatory paradigm, it must* meet the criteria historians of science have set out for evaluating such new ways of thinking. What is important to know about such rare occurrences and the information that is brought forward is that existing experts must rethink their well-honed bodies of explanation. Such a situation runs into considerable resistance from an "old guard," those who are academically steeped in the existing explanations. "Experts" are wedded to the status quo they know well, and often are closed-minded about explanations that do not come to light through traditional academic research channels, and from renowned academically positioned experts.[†]

What Thomas Kuhn, historian of science, found when he examined the examples of intellectual work that shifts the paradigm, is that completely new explanatory models must surmount mountains of resistance. New interpretive frameworks do seem to attract a small body of well-trained, intellectually astute young thinkers who accept the new model almost intuitively.

---

*The seminal work on paradigms and their effect on existing scientific knowledge comes from the research of Thomas Kuhn in his book, *The Structure of Scientific Revolutions* (1970). Notable among those whose work fell in this category are the books by Imanuel Velikovsky, *Worlds in Collision* and *Earth in Upheaval,* and the works of Australian scholar Barbara Thiering, Ph.D. Both of these scholars suffered serious criticism about their published findings.

[†]Several years after meeting Sitchin, and years after my study of his works unfolded, I published *The Legacy of Zecharia Sitchin* (Book Tree, 2011). The ingredients of a paradigm shift are discussed in that book. A notable case that grounds this last statement is made by the late Carl Sagan, who said that if a new planet was to be "discovered" coming to our solar system, he was going to be the one who discovered it, and he would be the one to announce it.

Perhaps this is because these students tend to be open-minded individuals who are in the early stages of forming their own world views. Most are newly trained to judge explanatory models on the merits of the data quality and the logic that informs the validity of the data. What also was found in the study of explanations that shift the paradigm is that these explanations slowly achieve more widespread acceptance as they become better known and are more thoroughly studied. Another thing that seems to be characteristic of the new explanatory frameworks: the old guard who mount the strongest criticisms and voice rejection eventually die out and leave a new generation of thinkers who do not have a full blown investment in the old way of making meaning to hold them back from acceptance of new, well-grounded explanations.*

One of the most provocative findings Sitchin made tells us how the modern human species came into existence. He bases his explanations on a close study of the tablet evidence. Here is a brief outline of his findings: To carry out the gold procurement mission, the Anunnaki toiled in the deep, dark, dirty mines of southern Africa. These workers developed a growing intolerance for the hard labor they were required to do. When they could tolerate it no longer, they collectively decided to rebel and carried out a mutiny. This stopped the gold supply to the home planet. However, the leader of the Earth mission, Enki, the chief scientist, and first to land on Earth, proposed a solution to the

---

*The process of legitimizing a body of new explanation (that shifts the paradigm) is further explained in *The Legacy of Zecharia Sitchin*. That book looks into Sitchin's scholarship, and examines the key contributions his research brought forth that covered new ground.

labor supply problem so that the mining could continue. Sitchin explains Nefilim inventiveness this way:

> Then, the Nefilim chief scientist came up with a solution. He said, "We can create a primitive worker, a Lulu-amelu, somebody who will do this work for us." When [the Anunnaki leadership council] said to him, "How will you create such a thing?" Enki, their leader, said that, and this is a quote from the text, "*This being already exists. All that we have to do is put our mark on it.*" Then the text, in great detail, described the process that the only modern parallel to it is that of bringing about test-tube babies. They mixed the genes of one of their young males with the egg of an ape woman . . . and after mixing the two, re-implanted fertilized eggs in the wombs of some of their own females.

> Now, some biologists and other experts in fertility tell me that this little detail [works]. The fact that I quoted it from the [ancient] text, that the fertilized eggs of the ape woman was re-implanted in the wombs of [Anunnaki] females who arrived on earth, let's say the ancient astronaut females, has great significance to the nature of the being that was finally created; that is very important. And, as we are Homo sapiens, not the hominid race which appeared on earth through evolution, but we [a new species] appeared only about 300,000 years ago through the efforts of someone who jumped the gun on evolution through genetic engineering.*

---

*This quoted material is from the Human Potential Foundation, *When Cosmic Cultures Meet*, 163–167. It is appropriate to point out that the Anunnaki female used is a bulbous female called the "Earth Mother." (See the color insert, Plate 6.)

This was Sitchin's short interpretation of the findings he derived from his intensive study and some thirty plus years of research into the ancient clay tablet texts. His research brought forward a *huge* body of information heretofore not explained in any other sources because he made use his space-age interpretative "lens" to unravel it from the ancient texts. Sitchin stayed close to the actual tablet records in all his interpretative work. He also urged more sharing of ancient findings, saying "The more we know and the more we discuss it, the better we will be prepared for the next encounter, and hopefully ensure a benevolent result."[3]

* * *

When I look back now to the nearly twenty years that Sitchin's work has informed my thinking and shaped my research, I am grateful for how much his work has impacted my life. I was able to travel with him and his groups to see additional examples of the evidence of the megastone structures the other terrestrials built that are found in several places around the Mediterranean.* I also was able to visit numerous ancient sites and museum collections I never could have found on my own. Along the way, I met people who shared the excitement of new learning I had come to appreciate, and developed good friendships with a group of Sitchin fans (scattered far and wide) who now enrich my life.

I am fortunate to have had numerous personal discussions with Sitchin throughout his later years and am able to call him a valuable teacher, a colleague, and a friend.† My first book, *The*

---

*Some of these places were the Trilithon, the huge stones of Baalbek that underpinned the landing site of Anunnaki vehicles, and the similarly huge blocks that underlay the ancient control center at Jerusalem.
†To highlight the personal relationship enjoyed by several people who were

Legacy of Zecharia Sitchin, was published in early 2011, barely a year after his passing.[†] It was unfortunate that Sitchin passed just as I was writing the final chapters of that book, but I did have the opportunity to discuss key points with him over lunch in June 2010, just before his ninetieth birthday.

This current volume searches out key contributions discussed in Sitchin's fourteen books published over his writing career (1976 to 2010). In it, I organize and unpack seven key topics drawn from across his entire set of writings. I selectively allow the reader to view his published information and point to his fuller published discussions as valuable resources. My goal is to report Sitchin's essential contributions and then interpret his evidence in light of today's trends and their implications for Earth's future. My process has left behind numerous other contributions his work covers, so reading his books will allow the curious reader to further enlarge his or her understandings.

The world now has the Sitchin books as a lasting body of evidence proving that a genius was among us for a few years short of a century. I trust this current book, highlighting, unpacking, and interpreting his findings, will provide readers with a glimpse into the man and his accomplishments.

Here we intend to provide readers with an opportunity to recognize that Zecharia Sitchin indeed brought the modern world a "gift from the gods" who ply the Universe. When they return as their planet traverses its "appointed" rounds at the end of its 3,600-year orbit, we will be able to understand who these first Earth settlers are and understand what our relationship is to them.

---

especially proud that Sitchin called them his friends, see the testimonials included in the afterword of my book *The Legacy of Zecharia Sitchin* (2011).
[†]Sitchin passed through the veil in October 2010.

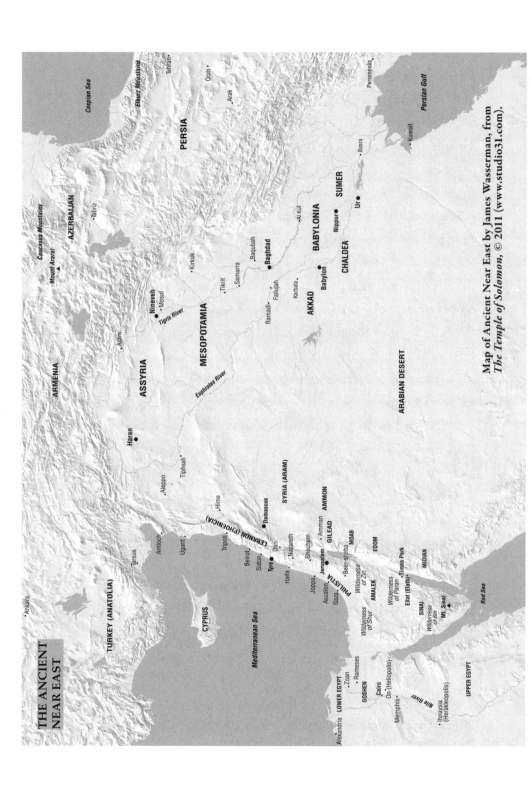

THE ANCIENT
NEAR EAST

Map of Ancient Near East by James Wasserman, from
The Temple of Solomon, © 2011 (www.studio31.com).

Introduction

Sitchin's
Space-Age Paradigm

When an explanation is given of something and
everyone in the world believes it,
there may be one person somewhere
who can't quite accept it;
who instinctively says—
"I'm not sure that this is sufficient explanation.
There may be something beyond this."

SPOKEN BY PIERRE CURIE IN THE MOVIE
MADAME CURIE, DIRECTED BY WILLIAM WYLER

Zecharia Sitchin was a highly intelligent twentieth-century man who probably for most of his life never thought of himself as the one who would shake up the accepted understanding of Earth's inhabited history and, more extraordinarily, enlarge the history of the origins of humans. But he did just that.

If we assign an overarching motivation to why Sitchin was so dedicated to this research work, beyond his belief that bringing provable ancient evidence into our modern mindset was important, it was his belief that "the events of ancient history will

1

have serious consequences for Earth's inhabitants *in the future*."[1] Sitchin firmly believed that *history foretells the future*. Most important, he was convinced that knowing about our ancient past would greatly benefit humanity.

Zecharia Sitchin was a man whose total body of work was orchestrated originally to add to the ancient symphony of information that slipped into contemporary times from its resting place in the desert *tells** of the Near East. As an innately curious man, Sitchin sought answers to difficult questions that arose from his probing research and study of works dealing with very ancient history. For example, when he followed his linguistically informed conviction that there was something beyond what everyone in the religious arena accepted as the correct interpretation of those called Nefilim, he found that the corrected translation of those individuals was "those who came down" (see the prologue). This corrected translation was the key to something very important. The answers he found revealed the true history of planet Earth: *who* came down, how they got here, what they did here, and what their former presence means for us—Earth's current inhabitants.

Curiosity and a strong motivation to find answers raised by the tablet records found in the tells (and elsewhere), prompted Sitchin to explore, in detail, the research of hundreds of published

---

Tells are mounds found in desert landscapes. They were sand-covered abandoned ruins, the remains of ancient settlements. One notable tell contained the library built by Sennacherib and Ashurbanipal, which contained clay tablets, stacked and catalogued, and preserved in the ruins of Nineveh. Some twenty-five thousand tablets, which proved to be copies of "olden texts," were taken from their resting place by Sir Austen Henry Layard. As related in Sitchin's *The 12th Planet,* these artifacts now are known as "one of great collections of Akkadian texts."

academic scholars, early historical researchers, and Sumerian scholars. After studying the existing sources, Sitchin taught himself to read the Sumerian cuneiform script and the languages that derived from it, namely Akkadian, Babylonian, and ancient Hebrew, so that he was able to interpret the original information for himself. He came to his study of Sumerian cuneiform script long after that language had been deciphered, transliterated, and translated. His research efforts led him to the museums and university collections where the ancient clay tablets were under study—or stored—and he traveled to numerous Near Eastern countries to see the ancient settlement sites.

When Sitchin learned to decipher the ancient scripts, in a language that used symbols (not letters), he was astounded to find words and phrases that suggested modern space-age concepts. It was then that he began to step outside the box of traditional explanation—*step to a different drummer*—because none of the interpretations put forth by traditional scholars appeared to be the *actual* meanings Sitchin found in the records. Using Sitchin's own words, we can see the nature of the problem that confronted many scholars who studied the clay tablets. His account clarifies their reactions to some of the implications of what they found in the ancient texts.

The discovery and understanding of the ancient civilizations has been a process of continuous astonishment, of incredible realizations. The monuments of antiquity—pyramids, ziggurats, vast platforms, columned ruins, carved stones—would have remained enigmas, mute evidence to bygone events, were it not for the Written Word. The ancient monuments would have remained puzzles: their age uncertain, their creators obscure, their purposes unclear.

We owe what we know to the ancient scribes—a prolific and

meticulous lot, who used monuments, artifacts, foundation stones, bricks, utensils, weapons of any conceivable material, as inviting slates on which to write down names and record events. Above all, there were the clay tablets: flattened pieces of wet clay, some small enough to be held in the palm of the hand, on which the scribes deftly embossed with a stylus the symbols that formed syllables, words, and sentences. Then the tablet would be left to dry (or be kiln-dried), and a permanent record was created—a record that has survived millennia of natural [deterioration] and even deliberate destructiveness.

In place after place—in centers of commerce or of administration, in temples and palaces, in all art of the ancient Near East—there were both state and private archives full of such tablets; and there were also actual libraries where the tablets, tens of thousands of them, were neatly arranged by subject, their contents entitled, their scribe named, and their sequence numbered. Invariably, whenever they dealt with history or science or the gods, they were identified as copies of earlier tablets, tablets written in the "olden language."

Astounded as the archaeologists were to uncover the grandeur of Assyria and Babylonia, they were even more puzzled to read in their inscriptions of "olden cities." And what was the meaning of the title "king of Sumer and Akkad" that the kings of these empires coveted so much?[2]

The original scholars had unearthed evidence of a very advanced Mesopotamian empire that existed in the third millennium BCE. They just could not understand this information within the context of their own society's development. The tablet records contained discussions of literature and art, science and politics, commerce and communications, all evidence of a developed civilization that existed long before Babylonia and Assyria. That possible notion was almost unbelievable. Sitchin recounts it in this way: "The scholars were incredulous: [they asked:] Could there have been urban centers, walled cities, even before Sargon of Agade, or even before 2500 B.C.?"[3] Sitchin's familiarity with enormous amounts of clay tablet writings allowed him to know that the answer to this question indeed was "yes."

Some of those ancient artifacts made references that had generated a strong *feeling of familiarity* for Sitchin in what was emerging as modern space-age science. How could that be? The tablets were at least six thousand years old. Sitchin kept this nagging feeling in the back of his mind as he continued his research. Finally, he figured out why some of the material prompted his "recognition." Those ancient activities were similar to modern scientific discoveries that were just beginning to penetrate modern societal understandings.

Sitchin's feeling of familiarity prompted him to enlarge his frame of reference, and likely energized his "what if" thinking. The Sumerian records suggested that these very ancient peoples had advanced technology in use long before the civilizations of Akkad and Babylon. That the tablets were describing space-age capabilities could not have entered the minds of the early scholars, and perhaps could not even have influenced modern scholars in the years Sitchin was carrying out his research that came forward in the publication of his first few books. Most importantly, the first scholars to decipher the tablet cuneiform scripts read the tablet material believing that what was discussed was mythological. Sitchin was able to unravel the full story of the ancient people's activities because he considered the tablet material to be actual ancient prehistory.

Sitchin sets out a creditable body of information that builds on the description of the first phase of Earth settlement, and this information sets the stage for his entire body of work. Using the tablets, Sitchin recounts that there was a time—the Sumerians told—when civilized man was not yet on Earth, when animals were only wild and undomesticated and crops were not yet cultivated. At that long ago time there arrived on Earth a group of fifty Anunnaki led by a leader whose name was Enki. They journeyed from their home planet Nibiru ("planet of the crossing"), and reached Earth, splashed down in the waters near the Persian Gulf. A text known to scholars as the "Myth of EA and the Earth" describes how that first group waded ashore, finding themselves in a marshland.

Their first task was to drain the marshes, clear river channels, check out food sources (found to be fish and fowl). They began to make bricks from the clay of the soil and established the first-ever settlement on Earth. They named the habitat Eridu, which meant, "Home in the Faraway" or "Home away from home." That name is the original of the name "Earth" in some of the oldest languages. The time: 445,000 years ago.[4]

Obviously, on the face of it, this material does seem to be a fantastic story. But, in museums Sitchin found thousands of clay tablets and pictograms (images carved on the hard material, in reverse, and rolled out on wet clay, which document the text they accompany). These cylinder seals—as they are called—produce a pictorial image that is used to illuminate Sumerian tablet text. Taken together, the tablet materials with the clay tablet pictograms led Sitchin to decide to put forward what has become a different, certainly provocative, and more accurate explanation of Earth's first settlements.

After centuries, the Sumerians (the "created" ones) became

the scribes of the advanced space travelers, recording information given to them by the Nefilim (the name the space traveler leaders called themselves). The stories recorded by the Sumerians who pressed cuneiform symbols into wet clay were *told to them* by what came to be known as "the gods of olden times." In essence, the Sumerians were like modern typists who take down what they are given and use those dictated "words" to create a final transcript. Subsequent civilizations copied the original information and put those stories, poems, and accounts into their own languages.

Samuel Noah Kramer, an early Sumerian scholar (who published before Sitchin's work came forward) believed the tablet information derived from the contributions of the Sumerians themselves. These contributions include the development and use of written script, kilns for baking clay (used for building structures), perfection of culinary arts from wide varieties of plants and domesticated animals, and the many "firsts" of civilized society—schools (teaching language, writing, and science), law codes, a bicameral congress, study of cosmogony and cosmology, astronomy, literary debates, and the study and practice of medicine, as well as the search for world peace and harmony.[5]

Sitchin, however, realized that it was *not* the Sumerians who developed the many civilizing features, but the Nefilim who *gave* humans these skills and knowledge as "gifts." Sitchin leans on Kramer's work to enumerate the scope of the civilizing features described on the tablets. Interestingly, even Kramer, who studied a plethora of tablets over many years, did not recognize the modern space-age implications held in those records.

Another important contribution made by Sitchin brought to our attention the link between the tablets—the record of an ancient history—and information laid out in the Bible. He explains this comparison source by telling us: "Since the biblical story of Creation, like the other tales of beginnings in *Genesis,* stems from Sumerian origins . . . the biblical tale is but an edited version of the Sumerian reports."[6] Identifying the Sumerian material as the source of the Bible's first book lends credibility to the historical truth of the Bible.

Why, then, were Sitchin's findings different from the tablet explanations already found in print? It is important to keep in mind that the redactions and translations of the cuneiform tablets *first* came into public view at the end of the nineteenth and early in the twentieth centuries, such as in the work by Rawlinson in 1861, King in 1896, Langdon in 1909, and other early scholars.

In Sitchin's ninety-year life-span, the world witnessed the birth of all of the achievements that give modern society its everyday and advanced technologies, and also its ever-expanding array of space technologies and newly developed scientific information. The technology array that emerged in Sitchin's lifetime includes a range of phenomena like airplanes supporting human flight, rockets and space vehicles that take people off this planet and into orbit, and space technology that can gather data from the edge of our solar system and beyond. In his later life Sitchin also saw the development of technology that can scan the outer reaches of our universe, and in his last few years, he witnessed plans to send humans to Mars.

It is important to realize that none of these technologically based space-oriented capabilities and their underlying concepts were even dreamed of when the first scholars struggled to understand the messages of space travel embedded in the ancient clay tablets. These ancient travelers were using technologies the world's modern societies only recently have invented. It was Sitchin's space-age perspective and astuteness that allowed him to

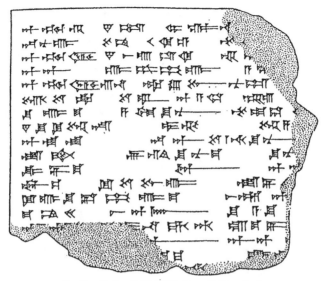

Creation Series, Tablet VII, ll. 1-18 (K. 2,854).

Fig. I.1. Tablet VII from the Tablets of Creation
(Enuma Elish) depicting cuneiform script.

understand what the early Sumerian scholars could not even see in the source material *because they were born too soon.*

When those scholars encountered tablet stories telling of beings using machines that could fly above Earth's surface with no restriction from gravity, or that a crew of spacemen encircled Earth in a spacecraft—allowing the astronauts on board to communicate back to Earth—such discussions would have been considered science fiction, insane fantasy, some sort of magical or imaginative thinking, or even prayers to an unseen heavenly entity. That the records discussed weapons that "zapped" targets (people) with a penetrating beam that brought death certainly is realistic in the twenty-first century, but described on arti-facts surviving from around 2024 BCE? Such content was more than fantastic; it was unbelievable. So the scholars did the best they could—they called all this type of information *myth*.

When Sitchin laid out the details he uncovered in his research, he was fully aware that his findings seriously departed from what had been published previously. He knew that he was treading on "unplowed ground" with his interpretations, so he carefully calculated the reaction that would ensue if—and when—he decided to publish his findings.

Sitchin's Courage to Publish

After years of intensive study, when Sitchin decided to publish the findings he derived from his analysis of these ancient materials, he revealed his considerable intellectual bravery. Sitchin had worked through thousands of clay tablets, journeying to museum collections in the Near East, Europe, and in the Americas, to study them with his own eyes. Through his work as a journalist in Palestine during WWII, he had developed superb organizational writing abilities, which he used to identify a first array of topics that he judged to be the most notable. In stepping into the book-publishing arena with his first book, *The 12th Planet,* he made good use of his well-honed journalistic skills. He knew the importance of using sources to support his research findings, so he carefully documented his text with the numerous sources he had worked through. However, his publishers forced him to reduce the number of references he originally prepared to include in that publication. These advisors believed that readers would be overwhelmed with a large amount of documentation, so Sitchin included only those sources that he deemed to be essential, those sources absolutely needed to ground his discussion.

That first book, published in 1976, proved to be a ground-breaking volume. The cover had this sentence printed on it: "Astonishing documentary evidence of Earth's celestial ancestors." With that sentence he tipped his hand as to the book's main contribution, and it attracted a global readership of those who were curious about the implications of that subtitle. The UFO crash in New Mexico in 1947 had raised the possibility of beings from another planet coming to (or near) Earth, and that UFO event inadvertently set the stage for Sitchin's discussions. In one sense, it was a precursor to Sitchin's first book in that it paved the way to the idea of "visitors from outer space."

In setting out information that probed previously uncharted territory, Sitchin made an important point in his "Author's Note" on the opening page of *The 12th Planet*:

> The rendering of Sumerian, Assyrian, Babylonian, and Hittite texts has engaged a legion of scholars for more than a century. Decipherment of script and language was followed by transcribing, transliterating, and finally translating. In many instances, it was possible to choose between differing translations or interpretations only by verifying the much earlier transcriptions and translations. In other instances, a late insight by a contemporary scholar could throw a new light on an early translation.[7]

I think Sitchin was referring to himself in that last sentence. As his research efforts probed deeper and covered an ever-widening scope of ancient and modern sources, he confirmed his early intuition that there was something else to uncover when he saw more and more clues of space travel discussed in the tablets.

He interpreted one sequence of Sumerian tablet records known as the *Enuma Elish** as telling (in a unique ancient style) of the existence and orbital behavior of *another* planet belonging to our solar system, which returns from deep space to orbit our sun approximately every 3,600 years. Further, Sitchin found that this other planet was—and still is—inhabited and those inhabitants were the ones who "came down" to Earth. They were the world's first astronauts, although that label was not the way they thought of themselves.

The information Sitchin uncovered from his own reading and translation of the cuneiform script was that these first settlers came in space vehicles to obtain gold and that they used advanced space technology to transship the gold they found here back to their planet. They had an environmental need for this substance; in pulverized form it was needed to preserve their planet's diminishing atmosphere. Sitchin's discovery gave us an understanding of humanity's passion for one of Earth's most precious resources—gold. Our need for gold is economic; perhaps its monetary value in modern society derives from this long-forgotten and very ancient environmental need.

Early in Sitchin's research process, it became obvious to him that he had amassed far too much material for one book, so he mapped out a series of topics that became outlines for five or six separate but related books. He called them "The Earth Chronicles." Over the next several years, he was a prolific writer. His findings eventually were contained in fourteen books,† each making a distinct contribution.

---

*This set of Sumerian tablets was first published by Leonard W. King in 1902 as *Seven Tablets of Creation.*
†Included in the Sitchin "library" are two books explaining details about the places he visited with groups of his fans. (See the bibliography for details.)

Sitchin believed that fascinated members of the public could observe for themselves the validity of his findings. Another of his accomplishments was to give these interested fans an opportunity to see evidence with their own eyes. First, Sitchin traveled to locate artifacts and structures in specific places that were referred to in the tablets, along with archaeological evidence now found in museums in the Near East, the Mediterranean lands, South America, Mexico, and a few special European locations.* Then he arranged and facilitated tours to those places, beginning in the early 1990s. See the color insert for photos from some of these tours.

The Challenges Confronting the Tablet Scholars

The early scholars who sought to unlock the secrets of the clay tablets faced many challenges throughout their research processes. First they had to reassemble what appeared to be rubble resulting from broken tablets. Extensive reassembly of the tablet shards was needed because many—if not most—of these clay artifacts had been seriously damaged when they were transported from the places in Sumer and Assyria where they had been found. Moving them from the sites in the field to the museums and universities who "owned" them was not done with a "white-gloved" painstaking approach. Many of the field workers were hired from local villages; to those locals, the "clay things" did not look like valuable sources of historical information. These irreplaceable records were tossed by the wheelbarrow-full into the equivalent of dumpsters

---

*Sitchin tours took fans to London's British Museum, ancient sites in southern Britain, as well as to Malta and Italy.

for transport. Few knew at the time that these bits of clay were priceless. The research effort required to reassemble the tablets and get them into readable form was formidable. Some of these restorative efforts continue today.

The largest body of tablet finds came forward in the late eighteen and early nineteen hundreds, and required intensive research efforts to reassemble them by the museums and academic institutions who sponsored the expeditions. Each of those organizations believed that what was discovered belonged to them; after all, they had financed the expeditions. Reports of these excavations typically were presented at prestigious professional gatherings and then put into print.

The study of clay tablet artifacts held even more challenges. They all needed to be decoded. The information they contained was in a symbolic form, written in what at first looked like strange wedge-shaped symbols. Intensive linguistic analysis brought to light that the etched lines on the clay could be translated into syllables that were the basis of a language, which we now call Sumerian cuneiform. As it turned out, this material proved to be the world's first recorded language.

The actual tablets found, for the most part, were *copies* of the original Sumerian tablets made by scribes in the civilizations that developed after Sumer and Assyria flourished. It is important to note that in the copying process, words were changed when the information was brought into the Akkadian and Babylonian vernaculars. These later scribes often substituted their own words for some of the original Sumerian ones. It was through this maze of complications and linguistic challenges that Sitchin worked to sort out the tablet stories and build his own understanding of their meaning.

Responding to Criticism

Doing his own translation and careful analysis of the tablets was the key to Sitchin's understanding of the true history stored on those clay tablets. While he was cognizant of the criticism that his work provoked, he never acknowledged it in print. It was Sitchin's strength of character that informed his refusal to acknowledge the negative voices that came forward and that still attempt to undermine the validity of his findings. It was his careful attention to detail and truthful adherence to the sources that gave him the unwavering confidence that his work was accurate and his conclusions were valid.*

Sitchin's published findings have been given considerable positive attention in North America, and in several countries around the world where several of his books are translated into some twenty (or more) languages. He was invited to meet with Msgr. Corrado Balducci, a representative of the Vatican, when he visited Rome in 2000 to discuss the Vatican's observation that Sitchin's findings did not threaten established views held by the Church.† In fact, he was reassured by this Vatican representative that his findings were highly acceptable in light of the concept of faith that permeates Church doctrine. It was pointed out by the Church's representative that if *reportorial evidence* is not acceptable as valid information, then the foundations of all religions must crumble.

---

*Interestingly, just before he passed in early October 2010, one of Sitchin's most dedicated followers met with him. Sitchin dictated several key understandings that he wanted his close friends to be aware of. One point he emphasized was that *all* of his writings stayed true to the tablet sources.
†Details of that visit are found in Sitchin's book, *Journeys to the Mythical Past* (2007) in the chapter titled "Vatican Encounters."

Fig. I.2. Sitchin with Msr. Balducci in Rome in 2000.

Sitchin was wholly confident about the accuracy of his research and the truth held in the evidence he found both in the records and on the landscape. Certain locations hold fascinating structures built by the ancient astronauts. One provocative example is found at Baalbek in Lebanon. It consists of a half-buried enormous stone block, partially shaped in its width and still buried on one end;

this is testimony to the fact that monumental stone undertakings were done by the Anunnaki (see Figure I.3 on page 18).

Because the civilization of which he writes was shrouded in unexplored (and perhaps previously unknown) history when he began to write about it, his published findings came as a surprise to contemporary scholars, and challenged earlier interpretations. However, this did not mean that Sitchin's work was incorrect. It represented a serious scholarly effort to delve deeply into records containing clues of the use of advanced technology and space travel. By the twentieth century, these records were scattered far and wide in museums and academic as well as private collections. Sitchin's publications represent a herculean effort to bring forward a coherent story of the first inhabitants of Earth.

The fact that his findings smacked of truth that, once deciphered, was obvious, is likely what threatened established interpretations and the personal judgments that accompanied them. Negative reactions frequently prompt establishment scholars to do one—or more—of the following things: to ignore the newly emerging work altogether, and to attack it as unfounded, incorrect, or unscientific; or to attack the man himself. In Sitchin's case, the criticism dealt with the fact he never was officially affiliated with an academic institution, implying he was uninformed about academic practice and about how to correctly use academic research and writing processes. Wrong! Sitchin grew up in an academic family, and he also undertook advanced study at the London School of Economics, a prestigious institution.

The implication of this critical stance is that his work was never *peer reviewed*. Within the academic tradition, it is the previously published literature that is the platform on which new findings are grounded. In Sitchin's case, after he read nearly

Fig. I.3. Baalbek, Lebanon: Huge trilithon stones that underpinned the landing site of Anunnaki spaceships, and a partially quarried block.

all of what was in print on ancient settlements and history, he realized that none of that previously published material contained any inkling that advanced space travelers came to Earth from another planet. That another planetary civilization made key contributions to Earth's cultural traditions and instigated humankind's progress throughout ancient history would have seemed preposterous. But to Sitchin, when he put all the clues together, it seemed totally logical.

Consequently we must ask how a peer review could be done by a reviewer who has no background in the substance of a topic (because no similar interpretation has been put forward in print), and the topic itself has no literature that can be used to ground it? The answer is that it can't be done. One only has to read Sitchin to see that he fully understood and carried out a well-grounded academic research process. His publications speak for themselves. His sources cover a wide range of topics appropriately selected to explain the content he discusses. The logic he uses to weave his new fabric of explanation is sound.

Recently even more attacks against the validity of Sitchin's work and accuracy of his word translations have appeared on the Internet. The Internet can be used to facilitate the promulgation of ungrounded negative views as well as legitimate criticism. Sitchin was one of two hundred scholars (in the world) who could read and translate the Sumerian language in the late 1970s, and who worked with the actual tablets. In doing his translations, he made use of his knowledge of Sumerian, Akkadian, Babylonian, and his understanding of Egyptian hieroglyphics. He also drew on his knowledge of ancient (as well as modern) Hebrew in order to work out specific word meanings. One has to wonder if the linguistic critics are as broadly competent. Did they study the actual tablets? Or did they use only the early translations and their interpretations that were written before the space age gave a key to the embedded meanings?

Sadly, it is unlikely that any of Sitchin's critics have read the full body of his work, looked into the quality of his sources, and observed how he selectively used previously published material to document his findings. We doubt those critical voices have followed his logic with their own careful reading of not only Sitchin's original work, but also the sources he used. Putting any of these verification techniques into motion likely would put to rest any critical assaults. If the linguistic criticisms that have come forward are posed by someone who reads Sumerian, has studied Akkadian and Babylonian, has translated Egyptian hieroglyphics, has worked in ancient and modern Hebrew, and who speaks German as well as Hebrew, and reads French, and of course works competently in English, then such a critic is qualified to launch criticism of Sitchin's linguistic interpretations.

One thing is for certain. Those who have identified themselves as negative Sitchin critics will find themselves on the wrong side of history as time moves forward and Sitchin's work is proved to be more and more accurate. Technologic advances already have brought to light information that supports his findings. As his ideas receive even more widespread recognition, Sitchin's numerous contributions will stand as a monument to his unbridled curiosity and his forthright use of his personal intellectual capability and courage.

Highlighting Sitchin Contributions

Zecharia Sitchin's work shakes up contemporary knowledge of science and cultural history. In this book's discussions, we celebrate several of his most valuable contributions, focusing on seven major topics pulled from Sitchin's fourteen books. In a real sense, this book is an interpretive biography of a dedicated scholar. While it focuses on Sitchin's work as an historian and archaeologist of ancient materials, it is designed to look at the man himself by penetrating his research findings: to first highlight and then interpret his reports* in the context of the twenty-first century technological capabilities.

One important understanding came in the form of the title of his first book. It contradicted modern astronomy's count of the number of known planets in our solar system. Sitchin counted twelve (based on the ancient records); contemporary science counted only ten (leaving out the Moon, which the Sumerians included). Publishing what appeared to be an obvious miscount, and as the title of a book, probably was Sitchin's first aggressive step; the second one was his decision to put his large body of findings into print.

Importantly, Sitchin's research findings also introduce us to the orbital behavior of the twelfth planet—Nibiru. In the ancient records, it is described as a planetary body four or five times larger than Earth, which returns to our solar system approximately every 3,600 years. This planet is absent from our portion of the galaxy for most of the time that it takes to make one revolution on its elliptical orbit out into deep space and then back into our solar system.

Sitchin found that the material on ancient cuneiform artifacts identified this planet as the home of the beings who came down to live on Earth in very ancient times. In the first two chapters of this book we will look at some of the important attributes and life-events of the foremost among the Anunnaki who came to Earth from the planet Nibiru, members of the celestial dynasty of

---

*Sitchin always referred to himself as a *reporter*.

the Nefilim.* By looking closely at Sitchin's research findings, we will learn of the activities and proclivities of those first settlers. We even will examine the motivations of some of these individuals as the ancient sources have explained them. These motivations (engines of action) hold implications for us.

Perhaps the most profound contribution of all those made by Sitchin is the explanation of the *creation of the human species* that we review in chapter 3. He provokes our thinking by posing this question: Was life *imported* to Earth from elsewhere? He then points out an astounding fact: life on Earth seems *not to belong here* as it "contains too little of the chemical elements that abound on Earth, and too much of those that are rare on [this] planet."[8] The seven tablets of the *Enuma Elish* introduce the fact, in an almost innocent way, that life on Earth was seeded here during cataclysmic primordial events that occurred during the processes that formed the solar system.

Sitchin points out that we are readily able to understand the behavior of the Anunnaki because *their gene imprints* are in modern humans. Sitchin discovered this in the tablet records.† The chief scientist of the Nefilim, Enki, knew how to use genetic science to "create" a blended being from an existing hominid living on Earth. He mixed genes from that source with Anunnaki genes. When Sitchin found and translated this information, he really covered new ground. This is the most provocative contri-

---

*The Nefilim, Sitchin tells us, were the leaders of the Anunnaki; the Anunnaki were the "rank and file" or workers of their society.

†In Sitchin's final book, *When Giants Walked the Earth,* he outlines a genetic research project he wanted to see carried out to identify Anunnaki genes in an ancient skeleton, but he passed beyond the veil before it could be accomplished.

bution he made as it highlights the use of genetic engineering in ancient times.

Sitchin's research opened up numerous other topics like Anunnaki love and lovemaking (examined in detail in chapter 4), as well as their space-travel technological activities, the focus of chapter 5. He tells us also of interesting interpersonal rivalries that spawned internecine warfare between Nefilim factions, so we take a closer look at wars and warring in chapter 6. The tendency of their use of warfare also included the first nuclear explosion on Earth that destroyed a key Anunnaki facility in the Sinai—along with the cities of Sodom and Gomorrah.* Those ancient events have meaning for Earth's future, now that those destructive technologies essentially have been "reinvented" in modern times.

Sitchin's research takes us deep into Earth's history, and out to the frontiers of modern science and astronomy—and beyond, as noted in chapter 7. All of this material will celebrate the work of Zecharia Sitchin, and in doing so, will enrich our understanding of who we are, why we are here, and where as Earth's inhabitants we are going.

Because we *all* now have an understanding of modern technological and space-oriented concepts, we, too, can understand what Sitchin recognized and what his insight told him were accurate explanations of ancient activities embedded in the tablet records. We can apply our modern knowledge to the space-related activities discussed in the ancient records. When Sitchin's 1990 book,

---

*It is reported that the "evil wind" from this explosion cleared Ur of every living thing, leaving only the buildings. Twentieth-century experience with nuclear explosions in Japan verifies this report from ancient times, as the same consequences are described as happening in ancient Sumer. See the appendices for more about these ancient nuclear explosions.

Genesis Revisited, came out, he raised an astute question on the book's cover: "Is modern society catching up with ancient knowledge?" We now know the answer to this query—yes, definitely!

Sitchin was convinced that his interpretations were backed by sound research and accurate use of sources—some obscure, but available to a persistent research craftsman like himself. Further, he was confident that his findings were supported by evidence anyone could use—if they had the willingness to prepare themselves by learning to read the languages of the ancient texts.

Sitchin reveals himself through his publications to be an undaunted researcher, a talented, engaging, and efficient writer, and a brave and confident author. His bravery was the essential character quality that enabled him to shift the explanatory paradigm. Those who strive to push the frontiers of knowledge forward would do well to take a lesson from Zecharia Sitchin, who is a first-class role model. He was that one person who was not satisfied with existing explanations, the one person who felt there could be something beyond the existing explanations. His contributions should be valued as his unique gift to those of us who now inhabit Earth. It now is our time to draw inspiration from Sitchin's incursions deep into ancient history. When we do that we will discover the future of humankind and the future of Earth.

The ark of rediscovery is sailing. It might be called "The Sitchin Ark of Discovery." Do come along for this informative and even exciting adventure as we explore in this book the ancient past Sitchin brought to light. That will enable us as modern humans to move forward on this planet, living in and contributing to an enlightened future.

1

The Astronauts
from Outer Space

When I approached Earth there was much flooding.
I approached its green meadows, heaps and mounds
were piled up at my command.
My house—its shade stretches
over the Snake Marsh.

REPORT BY E.A., FIRST NEFILIM TO LAND
ON EARTH 445,000 YEARS AGO, FROM
A TABLET FOUND IN THE RUINS OF SUMER

In an ancient long ago time, in an outlying part of the Milky Way galaxy, the planet rotating third from its star barely had emerged from an ancient ice age when it became the destination of a small group of space travelers—astronauts as they are called today—who had identified this planet as holding large amounts of gold. The leader of these astronauts was E.A., also known as Enki, a Nefilim, meaning "people of the fiery rockets" and "those who had come down." These space travelers were explorers, tasked by their king to land and carry out a gold procurement mission. Their home planet, Nibiru, had a diminishing atmosphere and pulverized gold was needed to rectify the effects of this problem. The planet they came to is now known as Earth. After surveying the lands surrounding the body of water into which they splashed down, the leader of this exploratory group had his "rank and file," called Anunnaki, build his residence on the banks of two major rivers that drained the uplands. There, from the bottom of the nearby water body (we now call the Persian Gulf), they began to extract gold.

This information comes to us from the diligent research of Zecharia Sitchin. Intrigued by the phrase "they came down" he launched a concerted effort to discover what it meant. His first research efforts focused on the Sumerian tablets, drawing on the early scholarly work of Austin Henry Layard (*Nineveh and Its Remains*, 1849), P. Jensen (*Die Kosmologie der Babylonie*, 1890), and George Smith (*The Chaldean Account of Genesis*, 1876). But Sitchin found that those first scholars were at a loss to interpret many parts of the tablet information. One particularly confounding problem for them was the fact that the information appeared on tablets that were scientifically dated to be six thousand years old. The conclusion that the early scholars drew was that they were reading about mythical and religious beliefs held by people who lived in very ancient times. Then Sitchin learned Sumerian so that he could re-translate the tablets. As he did so, he found that his own renditions revealed recognizable concepts, not legends, mythical stories, or religious beliefs, as the early scholars thought. The early scholars understandably were at a loss to recognize technologies that had not yet been invented in modern times. All the space-related concepts were totally opaque to them—but not to Sitchin.

Sitchin came to realize that the tablets were recounting the actual activities of the "ancient ones," the Nefilim and Anunnaki. But there was more. These ancient texts were discussing the landing and takeoff of space vehicles, communication between another planet and Earth, the use of flying vehicles for transportation from place to place, and the use of genetic science to create other beings. To further support his growing assumption that flying technology was in use in the very ancient times, there were pictographs that appeared to be illustrations of what was discussed in the texts. This material was the answer to Sitchin's lifelong questions about who came down.

What was particularly interesting to Sitchin, being a biblical scholar, was the fact that the ancient tablet records contained information that matched content found in biblical accounts, such as descriptions of a vehicle as a "'bird,' 'wind bird,' and 'whirlwind' that could rise heavenward while emitting brilliance, [which] leaves no doubt that [what] they were [telling about] were some kind of flying machine."[1]

In today's world, such observations and sightings, like those documented in the Bible, might be thought to be phenomena now called "unidentified flying objects" (UFOs). Modern sightings often have been considered by some to be the optical illusions of ground observers. In biblical times, reports of flying vehicle observations were made by notable people, like Jacob and Ezekiel; not only were their reports taken seriously, but they were considered worthy of inclusion in the biblical record. Jacob saw a "sky ladder" with beings going up and down, and Ezekiel saw a machine with "wheels within wheels."

Scholars will recognize this early information as *reportorial* evidence and might be inclined to suspect its veracity. Eyewitness evidence often is considered unreliable in today's world, where belief often is undermined with skepticism. Thus, the unbeliever might reject these biblical reports as hallucinations, dreams, or just weird imaginings. If those with a skeptical mindset read Sitchin's work, they will see well-documented evidence in support of the reality of these ancient observations, provided the Bible is accepted as an historical document containing actual history as well as theology. As Msgr. Corrado Balducci, a notable representative of the Vatican, told Sitchin, if reports of unusual phenomena were *not* acceptable as valid evidence in biblical times, then all of today's religions would crumble. Reports—then as now—were (are) the pillars upon which religious belief was (and is) based.

In the text of Sitchin's first book, *The 12th Planet*, in the chapter called "The Nefilim: People of the Fiery Rockets," he summarizes large amounts of data so he can reassure his readers that this evidence has widespread import. He tells us that pictograms that accompany the text are convincing documentation in support of tablet material. When did these convincing sightings take place? The ancient accounts tell us that flying objects were common sightings during the "olden days" when the ancient ones were on Earth. Sightings like those seen in the early days of Earth's settlement have continued throughout human history.* Sitchin lays out a space-oriented history of Earth's ancient settlements not previously discussed anywhere before Sitchin's books were published.

---

*Antonio Huneeus (in a Sitchin-edited book titled *Of Heaven and Earth*) was one of six contributors who delivered talks at the first Sitchin Studies Day, an event held in Denver, Colorado, in 1996. Those speakers provided evidence of a long history of flying vehicle sightings, much of it captured in artists' landscape depictions. His paper, titled "Exploring the Anunnaki— UFO Link" stands as the cumulating discussion linking modern phenomena to Sitchin themes.

The Settlements of Early Humans

Scholarly explanations that deal with how the first humans lived on Earth focus mostly on hunter-gatherers. The accepted descriptions indicate these people were seminomadic and lived in small family or tribal groups, mostly in caves.* These human groups were thought to be the earliest of Earth's inhabitants. Traditional scholarship of what we now call prehistory offered plausible explanations to support the lifestyles of these peoples, and artifacts (like stone tools) provided widespread evidence of how these implements improved their lives, especially their hunting (survival) efforts. In some coastal areas, especially Southeast Asia, longstanding ancient habitats were inundated, wiping out ancient evidence of settlement.† These impacts were the result of glacial melting causing sea levels to rise. Research also was complicated by interpretive conflicts between already published scholarly reports that contradicted findings.

When Sitchin published explanations of completely different (much older) ways of living, namely built-up settlements that gave rise to what we now know as urban lifestyles,‡ even though supported by tablet evidence, these findings were judged to be so unusual that they were disbelieved. Questions like this were highlighted: How could Stone Age hunter-gatherers develop such

---

*For example, in his *The 12th Planet* (17), Sitchin notes that a cave known as Shanidar, located on the side of a mountain at the headwaters of the Tigris River, was found to contain the remains of human occupation from about one hundred thousand to thirteen thousand years ago.
†See Stephen Oppenheimer, *Out of Eden: The Peopling of the World* (London: Constable & Robinson, 2004).
‡The oldest inhabited site in Anatolia is the Karain Cave located north of Antalya (a very large city on the Mediterranean coast), inhabited fifty thousand years ago.

complex ways of living? They reasoned that the evidence (or its interpretation) must be wrong. Obviously, very early hunter-gatherers could not have developed the features of civilized living, so *who was* responsible for such developments?

Here is Sitchin's answer: It was the technologically advanced Anunnaki who used flying technology for traveling through space. This urban way of life came from another planet. When Sitchin read the same tablets that the first scholars studied, in their original language as well as in redacted form, he realized the tablets held, in coded form, a wealth of information about ancient "gods" and the cities they built. It is important for us to know who the Anunnaki were and what they accomplished on Earth because their history is our history. In order to learn about those explorer-astronauts, we needed someone to study and interpret the records they left for us. Sitchin was that "someone."

The Story of the Anunnaki on Earth

The ancient evidence tells us that some 445,000 years ago, the first contingent of space explorers arrived on Earth to accomplish their primary purpose of identifying sources of gold and then extracting and processing the gold so that it could be sent "up" to their planet to be used to save the atmosphere there. The original group to come down on planet Earth was small; only fifty Anunnaki with one Nefilim leader. They landed somewhere in the Indian Ocean and made their way to the Arabian Sea, then northward to the marshy lands created by two major rivers, where they waded ashore in what we now know as Iraq. The planet was undergoing glacial melting as a consequence of climate warming, a natural process,[2] and the swollen rivers inundated most low-lying areas around the world.

As soon as they arrived at their planned destination, the leader of the mission, Enki, who was the chief scientist, immediately directed the workers to drain the swamps. Enki, who also was the firstborn son of the king of the home planet, Nibiru, had been appointed by his father to lead this expedition, next directed his house to be built. It was called (shown here in Sumerian syllables) E.RI.DU (House in Faraway Built). Sitchin tells us this became Earth Station I, and it was "a lonely outpost on an alien planet."[3] At those very early stages of Earth's settlement, Enki's several engineering skills and extensive knowledge of hydrology were put to good use. He focused on terraforming activities, directing the building of dykes and drainage networks, forging a connection between the two large rivers. This allowed the two river channels to merge, forming a larger channel that could be dredged. His efforts were successful in producing sufficient dry land for construction of a large settlement.

Historically speaking, Enki's early engineering successes were dwarfed by his greatest Earth-based challenge, which came much later. It was a challenge that reflected—to outside observers on his home planet—on the question of whether he was an effective leader of this extremely important gold mining mission.

When the explorer-astronauts turned their attention to the seafloor of the nearby large body of water where gold was to be found, this gulf seabed was mineral-rich. Gold was among the several minerals deposited there. However, the gold was so dispersed that, over time, the explorers realized it would not meet the volume needed to satisfy the gold requirements of the home planet.

A second gold supply site, in South Africa, was reported to be a rich source of the needed gold. There, gold indeed was plentiful, but it required hard labor in deep underground shafts to extract and bring it to the surface.* Then it needed to be transported by boat to the spaceport. All these tasks required large amounts of hard labor. When the gold mines had been in operation for a few thousand Earth years,† Enki was faced with a challenge that would be interpreted as a negative reflection on his leadership skills. The Anunnaki workers no longer wanted to toil in the deep, dark, dirty mines. Over time, these miners became extremely disgruntled over the harsh working conditions. They essentially staged a mutiny.‡ Enki, as the leader of this operation, had to face a disruption of the flow of gold required to supply Nibiru's needs. He was faced with what we today would call a serious confrontational labor problem and work stoppage. This crisis required a report to the home planet.

When Anu, the king on Nibiru, learned that the gold procurement mission was interrupted, he called a meeting of the high council of notable Nefilim then on Earth, and came down to Earth to arbitrate a solution. At that same time, he was facing serious dynastic problems on Nibiru. At the root of that problem was the fact that he had previously usurped the throne, and the deposed king's grandson was causing trouble over that issue. So Anu decided to bring Enlil, his second-born son, and the deposed

---

*A recent book discussing the South African gold mining area is Tellinger's *African Temples of the Anunnaki* published in 2013. (See the bibliography for full citation.)

†One year on Nibiru (known as a *sar*) was 3,600 years on Earth. Sitchin provides a likely timeline (in Earth years), which indicates that gold production in the gulf faltered 416,000 years ago. This timeline is found in *The Wars of Gods and Men*, 345–350. It indicates that the mutiny of the workers at the gold mines took place some 300,000 years ago.

‡Sitchin devotes his entire eleventh chapter to this event in his book *The 12th Planet*.

king's troublesome grandson with him on his visit to Earth.
Sitchin tells us:

> Both decisions, to take Enlil with him and also to take Kumarbi
> [the grandson] along . . . ended up making the visit one marred
> by strife and—for Anu—also filled with personal agony.
>
> The decision to bring Enlil to Earth and put him in charge
> led to heated arguments with Enki—arguments echoed in the
> texts so far discovered. This enraged Enki as it meant he lost
> control over the whole of Earth. The angry Enki threatened to
> leave Earth and return to Nibiru.[4]

Enki's problem was this: he had been operating on Earth as
founder and "commander in chief." When Enlil arrived, his very
presence indicated that Anu was changing the command structure
and putting Enlil in charge. Enki's resentment was expressed clearly
to his father. In spite of his angst, when the high council convened
and the labor problem was laid out, Enki volunteered a solution to
the king and the assembled Nefilim. He announced that he could
use his vast scientific knowledge to *genetically engineer* beings who
would be capable of performing the gold mining tasks.

Enki indicated that to accomplish the necessary genetic
upgrade, he would put an Anunnaki "imprint" on the hominid
that already walked about on Earth. Although this hominid was
deemed unsuitable intellectually for following directions—a necessary requirement for workers in the mines—Enki felt that this
hominid was sufficiently akin to the Anunnaki for this plan to
work. The hominid had been seeded on what became Earth when
the original ancient planet, Tiamat (Earth's name *before* she was
the victim of primordial collisions), had collided with Nibiru,

one of a series of huge celestial impacts. One of these catastrophes ripped the ancient planet in two, and another shunted it into a new orbital position, third from the Sun, thereby causing her name to be changed to Earth. The remains of Tiamat became further pulverized, and now are what we know as the "asteroid belt."

The outcome of the high council deliberations on the mining mutiny was that Enki was granted permission to genetically develop a "docile worker." With the assistance of the Nefilim's chief nurse, Enki's half sister Ninhursag, he worked to create a *lulu amelu* (primitive worker), a *helpful* worker (but not a slave), who would obediently work with the Nefilim and Anunnaki. Using the Earth-based hominid and genes from one of their own, Enki fashioned just such a willing worker. The success of this undertaking brought into existence a particularly noteworthy species—*Homo sapiens*.

What Sitchin's body of work tells us is very exciting. He reports that the beings created by the Nefilim—called "earthlings"—indeed were intelligent. Under Anunnaki tutelage they became scribes, accountants, astronomers, bricklayers, manufacturers, and scientists. They developed kilns and made bricks and built buildings (ziggurats); they were taught—and learned—how to grow grains and fruit trees; they learned to make beer; they kept meticulous business transaction records; and they even studied and read the stars. These earthlings were found to be so valuable to the Nefilim that they eventually were given the elements of civilization, and even kingship was transferred to a select few when the Anunnaki found noteworthy individuals. Obviously, *they were not slaves.*[*]

_____

[*]Several publications state that humans were created to be used as slaves by the Nefilim/Anunnaki. This is patently wrong. Humans were created with intelligence to be *helpmates.*

Sitchin begins his third chapter of *The 12th Planet* with these words:

> What was it that after hundreds of thousands and even millions of years of painfully slow human development abruptly changed everything so completely, and a one-two-three punch—circa 11,000–7400–3800 B.C.—transformed primitive nomadic hunters and food gatherers into farmers and pottery makers, and then into builders of cities, engineers, mathematicians, astronomers, metallurgists, merchants, musicians, judges, doctors, authors, librarians, priests?[5]

This question is as provocative as it is enlightening. Our discussion so far gives us the answer. The astute reader will recognize these dates as 3,600 and 3,200 years apart. That is the variation in the rotational interval of Nibiru's orbit.

Sitchin also unravels several Earth-based mysteries that have perplexed scholars and scientists, such as the origins of the huge unusual stone features seen on Earth's landscapes, like the Sphinx, the Great Pyramid, Stonehenge, Avebury, Newgrange, and hundreds of other structures made with huge multi-ton shaped stones. These huge artifacts have presented explanatory challenges to experts—archaeologists, engineers, and scientists— who have tried to understand *how they were* constructed, and w*ho* constructed them. As a result of Sitchin's diligent work, we now know that those who constructed many—if not all—of the huge stone monuments were the Anunnaki. As a result of Sitchin's research, we have new explanations for old questions, and answers that seriously enlarge our understandings. These are the characteristics of a shifted explanatory paradigm.

The Impact of Sitchin's Findings

As mentioned earlier, an approach to explanation that is more logical, more powerful, and interprets facts in legitimate new ways, uses a different mindset than already is in place, is not a new phenomenon in the history of science; rather, it is known as a "shift in the explanatory paradigm." Sitchin's work shifted the explanatory paradigm.*

Sitchin's close study of the records and related material provided him with the data he used to draw out the explanations we are highlighting here. A dedicated and fact-oriented journalist is trained to *verify* observations and information—not to merely follow hunches. Sitchin was just such a researcher. He also was a persistent researcher, who examined numerous reports and works of ancient findings from historians who published writings that are very difficult to locate.

It must be emphasized that it was body of well-educated scholarly individuals who had carried out the original expeditions and explorations, and thereafter published redactions and translations of the artifacts that were found and later studied. Their discoveries then became the substance of written reports that still today are used by some as the only legitimate sources. It was those previous works that provided Sitchin with the sources he read and re-translated. Sitchin made it blatantly clear he did *not* dig up the tablet artifacts, and then say, "Look what I found. This is what they say."†

---

*For a detailed discussion of the Sitchin paradigm and its impact, see chapters 2 and 4 of my book titled *The Legacy of Zecharia Sitchin*.

†This is an important point that Sitchin regularly brought out in his conference and seminar presentations. He felt it important for his audiences to fully understand that he *reported* what was presented in the traditional literature, but with a different, more accurate way of making meaning.

Sitchin was confident that the understandings he wrote about and talked about in his numerous presentations were accurate because he knew his research was thorough and his interpretation of the evidence was logical and substantiated in ancient facts. He confidently disseminated his research findings in print, at seminars, in conference presentations, and in a few radio interviews.*

As more and more of Sitchin's research work unfolded, he not only came to understand the technologic context within which those first Earth settlers lived and worked, but he also began to unravel the structure of their society, especially the leadership structure on Nibiru and its transplanted version on Earth. Sitchin learned who the key players in the Nefilim/Anunnaki story were and what roles they played—and expected to play—in their "home away from home." One of the important components of that "other planetary" society was how dynastic responsibility and power was passed from one generation to the next. These *rules of succession* became important harbingers of difficulties when they were applied to Nefilim offspring on Earth, generating problems that arose "in the beginning" when one of the first Nefilim to arrive on Earth struggled to adjust to why he could not inherit power over Earth and its inhabitants.

In the next chapter we will look at the Nefilim dynasty, identifying the individuals who came down to become the first Earth settlers and rulers. The information we have just covered is the first step in understanding Earth's developmental history. In the next chapter, we unfold the second step in understanding human history on Earth.

---

*Sitchin was heard, on occasion, on George Noorey's late night broadcasts, the talk show that followed Art Bell's popular "Coast to Coast" program.

2

The Anunnaki
Family Tree

There were many gods in Sumer—
children, grandchildren,
nieces and nephews of the Great Gods;
there were also several hundred
rank-and-file gods, called Anunnaki . . .
But only twelve made the Great Circle.

ZECHARIA SITCHIN, *THE 12TH PLANET*

Zecharia Sitchin made a most important contribution when he
gave us insight into the celestial dynasty of the Nefilim, beginning with a fresh interpretation of the references in the ancient
sources to "the Gods of Heaven and Earth, the ones called the
ancient gods. They also were called the 'olden gods' of the epic
tales."[1] A Mesopotamian inscription enlightens us further when
it states: "Whatever seems beautiful, we made by the grace of the
gods."[2]

Sitchin points out that archeological evidence supports what was written about the Anunnaki: they were powerful beings, capable of feats beyond mortal ability or comprehension. By comparison to humans, their stature and cranial features were enormous; they stood at least twelve feet in height, and reportedly had elongated crania. He describes them with these words: "these gods not only looked like humans but ate and drank like them and displayed virtually every human emotion of love and hate, loyalty and infidelity."[3] In fact, it is probably more accurate to say that *"we look like them* and *have similar traits and behaviors to those beings from another planet."* This clarification will become clear as this discussion unfolds.

The first scholars to translate the Nefilim/Anunnaki stories referred to the key players as "gods of olden times." Sitchin points out that in his writings he used the "god" label *only* because of its general acceptance, not because the Nefilim or Anunnaki thought of themselves under this label. The idea that Earth was under the direction of beings who were technologically more advanced, and whose stature was such that they had a commanding presence, has contributed to a belief system that the Anunnaki and Nefilim were godlike beings worthy of worship. In our judgment, their behavior did not warrant such reverence. They may have been honored because they were the teachers of skills that "earthlings" were thankful to receive, and because they exhibited technological knowledge, but the *concept of worship* as we understand it probably was not the way it was meant in ancient times.

Sitchin tells us that it was paganism that put the notion of divine beings into our cultural understandings.* The idea that

---

Culture is a way of thinking and believing, taught by one generation to the next, and is a powerful force that shapes belief and behavior. Traditionally, culture encompasses religion, language, and political ideology.

gods existed "up there" filtered into Greek and Roman beliefs, and obviously has its roots in the ancient Anunnaki stories. The understanding that gods existed on Earth—but came from above—persisted long after those entities left Earth.*

Sitchin's books provide us with a remarkable body of information about the individuals who comprised the Nefilim dynasty. His diligent and penetrating research gives us an essential history of these first occupants of Earth. His insights into the Nefilim are especially important because this information is not found— in the way Sitchin explains it—in any traditional literature, although discussions in more recent print and video materials are beginning to rectify this seemingly serious gap in traditional historical works.

Dynastic Rules

Sitchin noted that a total of six males and six females comprised the Supreme Pantheon or Great Circle of these "deities." The royal family consisted of a king, one daughter, and two sons (and eventually their offspring). Their hierarchy was defined by a numerical rank assigned to the males. It consisted of "the number 10 and its six multiples within the prime number 60." He briefly explains the numerical ranking system: they assigned the highest rank of 60 to Anu, the king of Nibiru, and subsequent ranks of 50 to Enlil and 40 to Enki. The wives of the dynastic individuals

---

*An enlightening explanation for humankind's current belief in a personal God or gods is that such a belief came from a cultural understanding that "the reason people invented gods is that they had *experienced* them! We are reminded that the *presence* and *their interest in humans* were felt." This quote appears in a 2011 book by Frank DeMarco titled *The Cosmic Internet*.

also were included in the Great Circle and given numerical rank associated with that assigned to the king and his male offspring, that is, 55, 45, and 35 respectively.[4]

Sitchin was able, by closely examining the clay tablet records, to help us understand the role each played on Earth. Preparing the landscape for occupation and the subsequent building of settlements was Enki's role. He also acted as the "shepherd of humans" after his "creation" efforts produced intelligent workers. Also, for some twenty-nine thousand Earth years,* he directed the important mission of the Nefilim and Anunnaki on Earth—the mining of gold.

Enlil, on the other hand, took over the gold transport mission and spaceport supervision, and administered the crucial communication linkage between Earth and Nibiru. He clearly was an "operations manager," and seemed to have little to do with humans, other than keeping order. Ninhursag proved to be a valuable peacemaker and mediator of rivalries that existed between her siblings. The king, Anu, did what kings throughout history have done—they oversee and make final decisions, arbitrate disputes, issue decrees, and carry out ceremonies.

The tablets tell that Enki experienced considerable consternation when Enlil arrived on Earth. To understand the reason behind his overt behavior at that time, we need to review the *succession rules* that were brought to Earth by the Nefilim. On Nibiru, dynastic power was passed from one generation to the next according to specific procreation rules. All members of the

---

*Keep in mind that an Anunnaki year (sar) is 3,600 Earth years, so their concept of time as it was lived on Earth was not as daunting as the number of years seems to imply.

ruling family were enjoined by these longstanding rules specifying who received the dynasty when a king either abdicated or died.*

Nibiru's succession rules stated that the *designated* heir—the offspring who would receive the ruling responsibility and hold territorial power and control over all major decisions within the domains in the realm—must have been conceived "properly" to preserve correct bloodlines. The ruling responsibility would be extended only to a "qualified" firstborn male in *each* generation—children and then grandchildren. In the case of Anu's progeny, only the son born to his half sister was eligible to inherit his realm. Whether within wedlock or not, a son born first, but *not* by the king's half sister, was *not* in line to receive the succession benefits, especially if a properly conceived second son came along.

Enlil was conceived by Anu with his half sister, Antu, which gave him the "right of succession" on Nibiru, and, eventually, on Earth. Before Enlil's arrival on Earth, Enki believed that Anu's dynasties would be apportioned so that each of his sons received a planet to rule over. He believed he would inherit Earth and Enlil would inherit Nibiru. But Anu must have made a deliberate decision *before* he left Nibiru to replace Enki as the "Lord of Earth," Enki's title up to that time. A mutiny had broken out at the gold mines and was the reason Anu had to come down. Could the mutiny problem have indicated to Anu that Enki's leadership was flawed, or lacked proper control functions, thereby permitting the problem at the gold mines to deteriorate to such a serious stage as to become a mutiny? We will never know the answer to this question, as Sitchin's recounting of tablet evidence

---

*Yes, the Nefilim and Anunnaki died, but after extremely long life-spans, unless by deliberate acts of violence or treachery.

does not give us Anu's reasons for his decision. We only can surmise that the underlying reason Anu made his decision as he did was because he lost confidence in Enki's ability to be an effective leader, and eventually to carry the full responsibilities of a king. Enki's authority might have been restored if Anu had taken Enlil back to Nibiru, but that did not happen.

The king's decision to bring Enlil down to Earth made it quite clear to Enki that his position on Earth was being usurped. Enki became so incensed with this decision that he argued with his father, and threatened to return to Nibiru. Sitchin tells us that Anu was afraid that if Enki went back to Nibiru, he would cause trouble there. The king's solution to this troubling situation was to arrange to have his two sons draw lots so that each would get a specified portion of Earth as his own domain: "Finally it was decided to draw lots: let *chance* decide how it shall be. The division of authority that ensued is repeatedly mentioned in Sumerian and Akkadian texts."[5]

In the drawing of lots, Enki got Africa, the continent that held the mining activity. This also gave him hegemony over Egypt, which included the Giza plateau's Sphinx and the Great Pyramid. This "acquisition" became very important later as Nefilim/Anunnaki history unfolded. With the domains on Earth assigned "by chance" and not by Anu's decision, the king could assuage his conscience. The drawing of lots was Anu's way of responding to the tantrum thrown by Enki. However, it was clear that whatever plans Enki had made for the earthly planet were erased; his position as "supreme leader" of all of Earth was over. When he lost his title, "Lord Earth," his name became E.A.

Enlil's presence on Earth not only raised jealousy and hostility between the two half brothers, but developed into an open rivalry, which played out through the next several generations. This intense rivalry of these two clans eventually took an unusual "twist" with an interesting joint decision made by the first generation offspring of Enki and Enlil. At a time of a pending crisis, a son of Enki and a son of Enlil joined forces against another son of the Enki lineage, Marduk, Enki's first-born son, who believed he alone was entitled to ruling power. When Marduk bragged about going after global power and taking control of the Sinai spaceport and all of Sumer, he acted on his belief that he was entitled to all the ruling power on Earth, but a coalition formed by a son from each clan worked out a plan to thwart him. This important episode will be unfolded later in this discussion.

The relationship between Enki and Enlil for centuries thereafter was tinged with all the angst and sibling rivalry that often arises within a privileged family, especially when a valuable legacy awaits the designated heir. When birthrights are at stake, and when the losing individual's future power to bequeath a valuable dominion to his own heirs is destroyed, a plethora of emotions ensue. It is just such a case that took place among the Nefilim on Earth.

ANU—Nibiru's King

The tablets report that Anu had for his kingly realm "the expanse of the heavens." He enjoyed occasional visits at his abode "up there" from Nefilim leaders (and even some mortals). These visits were for the purpose of the visitor to confer with him in his role as king, sometimes on individual issues, or when crises occurred on Earth.

Anu also came down to Earth to celebrate ceremonial events.

According to Sitchin's text, Anu came down for at least one ceremonial visit every 3,600 years (every revolution of Nibiru's full orbit), at the time when the planet Nibiru was approaching Earth's vicinity. Anu's ceremonial or state visits typically prompted activities of grand proportions. His house on Earth, located in Eruk, was so well appointed that the tablets describe it as having "irresistible charm and unending allure." It was called by the Sumerian name, E.ANNA (House of An), or "the house for descending from Heaven."⁶ For his ceremonial visits, he brought his spouse, Antu.

Anu's purpose for one particular visit was initially ceremonial, but also needed to resolve a dispute between Enki and Enlil. It took place after Enki lost his ruling rights over Earth. According to Sitchin's source,⁷ this visit held the specific purpose of hearing a strong objection voiced by Enlil against Enki. For the ceremonial event, the seating positions of the Nefilim royal family are detailed in the tablet text (notice Enki is not mentioned):

> the occasion was a visit . . . for one of those deliberations that determined the fate of gods and men on Earth every 3600 years. . . . Anu sat on the seat of honor, near him sat Enlil; Ninhursag [his daughter] sat on an arm chair.⁸

What Sitchin observed from a close study of the tablet materials was that Enki planned to undertake a huge refurbishing effort to restore his flood-ravaged city, Eridu, so it could continue to be his residential city. This was to take place well after the Great Flood (the environmental event placed by Sitchin's timeline to be eleven thousand years ago). According to the Sitchin-constructed timeline,⁹ this effort to rebuild cities took place about 7,400 years ago. Part of the dispute launched at the outset of the discussion with Anu was that all the other cities inhabited by Anunnaki also wanted the same rebuilding opportunity but did not want to wait until some indefinite time in the future to implement the rebuilding activities.

Enlil voiced a complaint to Anu against Enki's decision to focus first on his own city, because the reality was that Enki did not want to disseminate some special information—*Divine Formulas*—he held control over to Enlil and the other Nefilim. Enlil made accusations against Enki about withholding this valuable information that contained more than one hundred aspects of civilization (not specifically identified) that Enki would keep in Eridu. When Anu heard the case presented, he proffered this decision: "Enki must share the *Divine Formulas* with the other gods, so that [the other gods], too, could reestablish their urban centers."[10] In other words, the elements of civilization were to be granted to the whole of Sumer by edict of Anu.

In several of Sitchin's books, bolstered by the work of the University of Pennsylvania scholar Samuel Noah Kramer,[11] Sitchin indicates that the elements of civilization were reported to have appeared "suddenly." If the elements of civilization to which Enlil referred were the same ones that were identified by this Sumerian scholar, then this was an important body of information for both the Anunnaki and earthlings. Enlil's complaint, however, may have been motivated more for the purpose of appeasing the other "gods" who wanted this information to develop their own cities more than to give earthlings the benefits of civilization.

The outcome of the dispute was a proclamation by Anu. He decided to order Enki to release the formulas so that all of Sumer could benefit The decision to share the information about civilization's attributes gives us an insight into Anu's role as "supreme" decision-maker and ruler of the Nefilim and the Anunnaki, both on Earth as well as on Nibiru.

Interestingly, no pictorial imagery has been found in any of the numerous tablet collections depicting the personage of Anu. Sitchin mentions that several of the elements of the ceremonial sequences held around Anu's visits are recognizable on tablet pictorial depictions. But no cylinder seal pictogram is found in Sitchin's works identifying Anu himself. While the *sign* of Anu was a star that stood for "heaven" and "divine being," and was used in written cuneiform text, his *insignias* were the tiara (the divine headdress), the scepter (symbol of power), and the staff (symbolizing the guidance provided by the divine shepherd). We can see these identifying symbols of kingship still used in religious and royal pageantry to this day, such as that of the British royalty at weddings and other royal ceremonies. Is it possible that the use of these objects in royal processions derives from very long-standing practices begun in olden times by the Nefilim?

ENKI—First Nefilim on Earth and the Benefactor of Humans

Enki, whose name at first meant "Lord Earth," was given this designation when he landed on Earth. This was his name in his role as leader of Earth's settlement process and when he held full responsibility for Earth's development. Sitchin tells us that Enki was a brilliant scientist and engineer; because of his expertise, he also was known by the nickname NU.DIM.MUD, which means "He Who Fashions Things."

Enki was Anu's firstborn son on Nibiru, and was born of a not-frowned-on liaison by Anu with one of his six concubines.

While there was no censure of a king having the sexual "services" of concubines, that alternative liaison affected Enki by negating his position and future legacy under the rules of succession, particularly after Enlil was born by Anu's "proper" relationship with Anu's half sister.

When Enlil came to Earth Enki's name was changed to E.A. (Whose House is Water). Sitchin tells us that E.A. appeared to have accepted Enlil's succession status, but some who have studied the tablet evidence closely believe a power struggle continued between E.A. and Enlil (and may have continued well into Earth's history). Sumerian scholar Samuel Noah Kramer titled one of the ancient texts he studied "Enki and His Inferiority Complex."[12] Kramer's choice of words for the title of this tablet speak volumes about Enki's behavior.

Enki held the requisite skills and knowledge that supported his work as a master engineer and hydrologist. As mentioned earlier, Enki's first terraforming activity was to build a great house, called E.RI.DU (Home of Going Afar) on land raised well above the water level. Sitchin tells us that another translated tablet text was named the "Myth of Enki and Eridu" by Samuel Noah Kramer. It chronicles Enki's building project:

> *The lord of the watery-deep, the king Enki . . .*
> *Built his house. . . .*
> *In Eridu he built the House of the Water Bank. . . .*
> *The king Enki . . . has built a house:*
> *Eridu, like a mountain,*
> *he raised up from the earth;*
> *in a good place he had built it.*[13]

Great pains are taken in the Sumerian texts that Sitchin highlights to discuss Enki's house, "which remained Enki's seat of power and center of worship throughout Mesopotamian history" and "was built on ground artificially raised above the waters of the marshlands."[14] After landing on Earth, he also is reported to have built dikes to control incoming water from the Tigris River. Sitchin tells us that Enki's water-related affiliation was the forerunner of the Greek adaptation of that role (centuries later) as Poseidon.

The underlying theme of Enki's relationship to water, though not identified in more than a few words, was his concern for having a potable water supply to sustain life for all the occupants of his household ("gods," humans, and animals) and his landed holdings—the gardens and orchards. Having a sufficient safe water supply for consumption and for irrigation of plant-based foods was important for survival. Enki's worry about water quality was well founded because in regions like Sumer, where rain is forthcoming only in cool weather, irrigation using good water was—and is—necessary to keep gardens and food-bearing tree crops alive in the spring and summer growing seasons.

If one reads the text carefully, with an academic eye, it reveals that Enki was what we now call an hydrologist. His knowledge of water behavior on the landscape is notable as it made it possible for him to change the landscape to rectify flooding problems. Of necessity, he also developed the knowledge we today associate with a climatologist, one who understands long-range patterns of fluctuations in rainfall, temperature, and wind patterns, and the ability to use these data to predict storms.* He, without doubt, understood

---

*The distinction between *climate* and *weather* is clarified by academic definitions that are pertinent to this discussion. Whereas *climate* is the long-range trajectory of temperature patterns, average rainfall amounts, and seasonal frequency, *weather* is the day-to-day vicissitudes of these same variables coupled with wind patterns.

that getting control of surface water was imperative for the health of the earthlings and for the Nefilim as well. Swampy surface waters are a breeding ground for mosquitoes and other insects, some causing disease, as well as for aquatic creatures who thrive in sun-warmed water collecting basins. Sitchin points out that Enki was responsible for purifying the waters of the Tigris river, and building a canal to allow a connection between the Tigris and Euphrates rivers in their lower reaches. These hydrologic projects were Enki's efforts to control surface water inputs to the delta to alleviate the swamps. They were feats of engineering that became characteristics of Enki's dedication to making his own and the other Earth-based settlements of Sumer into thriving and sustainable habitats.

Enki held still another responsibility: he was in charge of the Moon, perhaps stemming from the fact that the Moon is related to tides. According to tablets written in the first person, Enki also took credit for introducing the plow and yoke, building the stalls and erecting sheepfolds, bringing to Earth the arts of brick-making for building cities and dwellings, and for metallurgy.*

Sitchin celebrated Enki by putting what he believed was Enki's first-person report, preserved through history as a long narrative poem, into a separate book that he titled *The Lost Book of Enki.*†

---

*The Sitchin evidence reports that Enlil and Marduk (Enki's son) also claimed credit for introducing the plow and yoke, building the stalls and erecting sheepfolds, for brickmaking, and for metallurgy, indicating the noteworthy nature of these accomplishments and explaining why other Nefilim also wanted credit for these developments.

†This Sitchin book, published in 2002, differs from Sitchin's usual style of writing. It takes the form typical of Sumerian tales with the characteristic repetitious sentences. Sitchin does not label this work a novel, but likely it is just that. It also may have been smoothed out (and perhaps filled in) with his interpretation of what Enki would have said if the source had survived in perfect condition. See bibliography for full citation of this autobiographic book.

Drawing together this first-person account contained on a nearly perfect set of Sumerian tablets, Sitchin, allows the "voice" of Enki to relate his own activities. Scholars called the original Sumerian text "Enki and the Land's Order."

Perhaps the most noteworthy accomplishment of Enki or any of the "ancient ones" was the creation of earthlings by genetic engineering. This event is of monumental importance to the development of Earth and certainly is notable to us, the humans who form his legacy. The Sitchin discussion of this contribution by Enki and his half sister Ninhursag is so important that we will unfold it separately, in chapter 3, so its details can receive full attention.

Another and perhaps the most unique contribution made by Enki involved his creative way of saving a small seed of humanity in the face of what the Bible refers to as the Deluge and history calls the Great Flood. The ancient texts give us additional insights into this biblical story.

Enki was privy to discussions in an important Nefilim gathering called the Assembly of the Gods (Sitchin's words), a gathering called by Enlil after he received a report from the Igigi, those Anunnaki astronauts circling and monitoring Earth from spaceships. This report told of the increasing instability of the ice sheet on the landmass of Antarctica. The report predicted the ice sheet would be completely destabilized by Nibiru's upcoming return to Earth's vicinity on its orbit around the Sun. It was predicted to slide into the southern oceans, no doubt indicating that it would create a huge tsunami that would seriously inundate the landmasses bordering the vast Indian Ocean. The extensive area predicted to be inundated constituted the inhabited lands of the Anunnaki and all the human settlements as well.

Enlil enjoined the Nefilim and Anunnaki to keep this information from the humans. Under the oath he demanded they adhere to, no Nefilim was allowed to *tell* humans about the upcoming devastating event. The Nefilim and Anunnaki were ordered to assemble at the spaceport (at Sippar) so they could "lift up" to safety in their spaceships when the Deluge hit. But the humans were expected to perish. Enki at first held back his vow of silence. Then he was forced to agree with the Nefilim rule that required him to obey Enlil's edict. However, Enki simultaneously began to figure out how to save a few of those humans he had created.

According to tablet records, the majority of earthlings had been engaging in behavior that seriously upset Enlil; it was said that the humans had gotten out of hand,. He regarded this natural disaster as a way to accomplish his vengeful desire to eradicate all earthlings. The issue that was foremost in Enlil's list of grievances against the burgeoning population of humans was that several Anunnaki "saw the daughters of men as beautiful and married them." Enlil believed that intermarriage of Anunnaki and humans was immoral.*

Enki, on the other hand, had various reasons for *not* wanting humans to be purged from Earth, the most important being that humans were his creations. Sitchin believed that Enki held genuine affection for many humans. Although Enki was enjoined by the Nefilim rules of the Assembly of the Gods, and therefore forced to keep his oath of silence, he creatively figured out how to do both—follow Nefilim rules to keep his pledge of silence *and* save a very small handful of humans. Enki, being the resourceful

---

*The full story of Enlil's disgust with what he considered to be the immoral behavior of humans is given in Sitchin's *The 12th Planet,* 347–55.

plotter that he had proved to be in other endeavors, figured out a solution that would communicate his plan to one of his favorite humans, Noah the priest. He designed a way to give Noah instruction on what had to be done, giving no reasons, just directives. Enki held a special regard for Noah who was "a righteous man . . . of pure genealogy."[15]

Noah was known in the tablets also as Utnapishtim, Ziusudra, and Atra-Hasis. He was a priest who followed religious practices faithfully as demonstrated by his regular visits to temple for prayers several scheduled times each day. Enki made sure that he arrived at the temple just before Noah at one of those scheduled times. He then went behind the curtained altar, and sat down looking at a wall. He began to talk (to the wall) as Noah entered. Noah thought he was hearing the "voice of God," and listened intently. Enki told (the wall) of the coming flood, and began giving dimensions for the building of a "submersible" ark to be built in a very short period of time. He also told the wall that this submersible vessel was to carry the seed of all living things (not the actual animals, just their seed) for use in replenishing Earth after the Deluge. Only a few live animals needed for food were to be carried onboard the vessel. The only passengers on this vessel were to be Noah's family and a navigator who was to assist Noah as the floodwaters dissipated to locate the landing site that Enki had designated. The navigator would be needed to locate the highest peak in the northern part of Mesopotamia, a high altitude location that would emerge first from the receding floodwaters. History tells us that the selected location was the area of the twin peaks known at Mount Ararat.

While the remnant humans were in a watertight ark, built to Enki's specifications, the Nefilim and some Anunnaki were huddled in multiple spacecraft aloft, eventually becoming thirsty and hungry. Some of the females wept when they looked down at the tumultuous waters. The sight of earthlings drowning in the roiling waters on the Earth below their craft was emotionally wrenching. The Sitchin text tells us that having to leave the planet's surface, the Nefilim "suddenly realized how attached they had become to it and its inhabitants. . . . Ishtar [Anu's granddaughter] cried out "The olden days, alas are turned into clay;" the Anunnaki who were in her craft "wept with her."[16]

When the waters receded, the ark was safely guided to land on the taller of the two Ararat peaks. Sitchin's words are clearer than any paraphrase would be, so we will use them to relate the landing event. A sacrifice was offered by Noah's entourage to celebrate their thankfulness for being returned safely to dry land:

> As soon as Atra-Hasis [Noah] had landed, he slaughtered some animals and roasted them on a fire. No wonder that the exhausted and hungry gods "gathered like flies over the offering." Suddenly they realized that Man and the food he grew and the cattle he raised were essential. "When at length Enlil arrived and saw the ark, he was wroth." But the logic of the situation and Enki's persuasion prevailed; Enlil made his peace with the remnants of Mankind and took Atra-Hasis/Utnapishtim in his craft up to the Eternal Abode of the Gods.[17]

Enlil, after becoming pacified by Enki and others, is reported to have reconsidered his vengeful attitude. In his (we presume) remorse, he utters a well-recognized (biblical) statement: "Go forth and multiply."* Enlil realized that earthlings were invaluable to the Nefilim and Anunnaki, and he decided that humans should be commanded to repopulate Earth.

One has to wonder: if only Noah and his three sons were aboard the ark (as is typically reported), how could Earth be repopulated? Sitchin must have faced this same question. Where would females come from to provide procreation capability? In his search for clarification, Sitchin found an account by the historian Berossus that tells the story. It reveals that "at the last moment friends or helpers of Ziusudra (and their families) also came on board," and after the ark landed, as the report goes, these "other people were given directions to find their way back to Mesopotamia."[18] If this historian's report is true—and it certainly is logical—it is just one more example of how diligent Sitchin was in dealing with issues that were reported in the records that were in need of logical clarification. He searched until he found answers in obscure sources.

For his assistance and benevolence to humans, as well as his many other accomplishments, Sitchin tells us that Enki was "Mankind's greatest benefactor."

ENLIL—The Most Powerful of the Nefilim

Enlil was viewed as the most formidable son of Anu, not just because of his birthright, but also because of his leadership style. Sitchin tells us that his name meant "Lord of the Airspace." He

---

*Although this phrase appears in Genesis 9:7, implying that it was spoken by the monotheistic God, it was said by Enlil to Noah on Mount Ararat. The Bible's text says only this: "As for you, be fruitful and multiply. Populate the earth abundantly and multiply in it. Then God spoke to Noah and his sons."

also held the title "Lord of the Command," which often is nar-rowly interpreted to focus only on his responsibilities to manage the spaceport. The scope of his role in that command function was seriously enlarged after Earth's domains were assigned by the drawing of lots. However, Enlil's domain encompassed all of the landmasses north of the Mediterranean Sea and Indian Ocean.

Enlil also held the prestigious position of leading the sessions of the high council, a responsibility given to him by Anu. Enlil pre-sided over those gatherings alongside his father, Nibiru's king. That position beside Anu signified his assigned power. Those meetings were held in the divine precinct of Nippur, the city where Enlil resided. Tablet records tell us how much he was revered:

> *Enlil,*
> *Whose command is far reaching;*
> *Whose "word" is lofty and holy;*
> *Whose pronouncement is unchangeable;*
> *Who decrees destinies unto the distant future . . .*
> *The Gods of Earth bow down willingly before him;*
> *The Heavenly gods who are on Earth*
> *Humble themselves before him;*
> *They stand by faithfully, according to instructions.*[19]

Obviously all those around him not only respected Enlil's position, but showed acquiescence to his leadership, which mani-fested with a stern and unyielding style. It was entirely possible that those he commanded feared him because of his uncom-promising manner. The Anunnaki called him "Ruler of All the Lands," and made it clear that "in Heaven—he is the Prince; On Earth—he is the Chief."[20]

One of Enlil's most important responsibilities was his command over the "bond heaven-earth." This "bond," called DUR. AN.KI, was some sort of technological connection between Earth and Nibiru. Perhaps it was a voice transmission technology such as modern space explorers who went to the Moon used to communicate with mission control. Remember the now famous message: 'Houston, the Eagle has landed"? This Anunnaki technology also included the application of information from celestial charts and orbital data displays called the Tablets of Destinies. The functions of these tablets obviously were complex. Therefore we surmise they used a very special and powerful computer. Sitchin tells us that all of these space-related control functions were monitored and directed from Enlil's mission control center in Nippur, and it was where the "comings and goings by the space vehicles and communications between Earth and Nibiru [were maintained], while both planets pursued their own destined orbits."[21]

It was said also that Enlil could "raise the beams that search the heart of all the lands—eyes that could scan all the lands."[22] What this sentence refers to is not explained further in the tablets Sitchin used as his sources, but these descriptions remind us of some recently developed modern technology. Could these descriptions be referring to something like the HAARP technology (High-Frequency Active Aural Research program) that emerged in the late twentieth century? Developed in 1990 by the U.S. Air Force, HAARP is a radio beam array system that sends beams skyward (to bounce off the ionosphere). These beams are not light beams, but microwave frequencies that excite areas of the ionosphere, supposedly to increase the *accuracy of communication* and also for surveillance. This technology has been linked (by critics) to control of Earth's weather.

Another possible analogy to the Anunnaki Earth-scanning capability is the Google Earth satellite scanning technology. While we have no detailed ancient descriptions from which to draw accurate or even approximate parallels, Sitchin's belief that modern science is beginning to develop technologies that were like those in use in ancient times is intriguing, and perhaps extremely informative. What we know now for certain is that the Anunnaki did have advanced technologies and we modern humans probably only recently are arriving at a similar level of inventive technological capability.

One important event in Enlil's life points out that, even with the level of power that he held and received recognition for, he was *not* above the law. He committed a major moral (sexual) transgression against a young Anunnaki woman and received punishment for it. This punishment tells us that the Anunnaki code of conduct treated leader and rank-and-file alike. We will discuss this interesting sexual event involving Enlil in chapter 4 when we explore love and lovemaking proclivities among the Nefilim.

NINHURSAG—Anu's Daughter

Ninhursag was a Nefilim born on Nibiru, as were her two half-brothers, Enki and Enlil. In the characteristic fashion of Anunnaki multiple naming practices, Ninhursag (Great Lady) also was known as Sud, Ninmah, Ninti, and Mammi. She was the nurse who was in charge of Shuruppak, the Nefilim medical center. Her largest claim to fame was her partnership with Enki in the genetic development of the primitive human workers. A tablet reference tells us that one day, while working in the lab on that project, she "got drunk and called over to Enki,"

How good or how bad is Man's body?
As my heart prompts me,
I can make its fate good or bad.[23]

After producing several imperfectly functioning "miscreations," Ninti (her name as the Lady Who Gives Life) finally created a perfect human specimen. Sitchin recounts that with these words:

This being was so much akin to the gods that one text even went so far as to point out that the Mother Goddess gave her creature, Man, "a skin as the skin of a god"—a smooth, hairless body, quite different from that of the shaggy ape-man.[24]

Looking at another episode in Ninhursag's experiences captured on tablet records, we find that when word came of the coming Deluge, Enlil called all Nefilim to Sippur so they would be prepared to board spacecraft to lift off when the tsunami arrived. Ninhursag was among those who boarded a craft to ride out the storm from above. She observed the devastation as the Deluge swept away all things in its path, drowning multitudes of earthlings below. She was shocked by the utter devastation. A tablet record tells us

The Goddess saw and she wept . . .
her lips were covered with feverishness . . .
"My creatures have become like flies—

> *they filled the rivers like dragonflies,*
> *their fatherhood was taken by the rolling sea."*[25]

By the time the tumultuous seas subsided, Ninti's creations were gone.

Ninhursag/Ninti also made a brave and notable contribution as the peacemaker who ended the vicious war known as the Second Pyramid War. This conflict pitted Enki-ites against Enlil-ites over control of the Sinai spaceport. The Giza area was under Enki's control, given at the time of the partition of Earth territories by Anu. However, it later became occupied by Enlil-ite forces when the Sinai was coveted because it held the spaceport. Ninurta (Enlil's foremost son) took up the challenge to wrest the Sinai from what he called "the usurpers." This war, including its final battle, was fought in Giza, and was led by Enlil. The battles of what are known as the Pyramid Wars were "vicious and ferocious" according to reports, and during those wars Ninurta's "Brilliant Weapon" caused horrendous devastation. It could blind a victim. It also likely held nuclear warheads.

In her efforts to bring the Pyramid Wars to an end, Ninhursag decided to enter the Great Pyramid to entice Enki (who had taken refuge there) to leave. Ninurta was astounded by Ninhursag's decision to "enter alone the Enemyland." But she had made up her mind to engage Enki who was inside this giant structure. Ninurta gave her the protective clothing needed to shield her from lingering radiation* produced by the beams that he had used inside that structure. She shouted to Enki as she neared the Pyramid, and the text says, "she beseeches him." Enki agreed to surrender,

---

*This was the first, and perhaps only, reference to nuclear radiation from Ninurta's Brilliant Weapon that we found in the weapons Sitchin discusses.

but with a condition that a final resolution of the conflict needed to come at "the destiny-determining time."* The Mother of the Gods, Ninhursag, took Enki by the hand and led him out of the Pyramid, along with the other defenders. Sitchin's words then were: "Ninurta and his warriors watched the Enkites depart."[26] Ninursag conducted Enki and the other defenders to her abode in the Sinai, called the Harsag. At her hand, the brutal war was over.

Ninursag had been given the Sinai when the other domains were assigned to her step-brothers, and she suffered great anguish when the nuclear event of 2024 BCE† focused on the spaceport located in her domain and annihilated this most vital structure. Obviously this disaster made the larger domain of Sinai itself unlivable (see appendix B for explanation of "The Evil Wind").

The Subsequent Generations—Nefilim Offspring

Both Enki and Enlil had sons who were notable in Nefilim history. Enki's sons were Marduk, Nergal, Gibil, Ninagal, and Dumuzi.‡ Enlil's sons were Ninurta, Sin, and Ishker/Adad. We will highlight here only those of the royal offspring that received considerable attention in Sitchin's work.

Enki's Son, Marduk

Enki's firstborn son, Marduk, was an egotistical Nefilim who made numerous decisions that caused all sorts of tribulations, both for his family and himself. Before the Deluge, he told his

---

*No further discussion is given to explain the meaning of this comment.
†This nuclear event will be discussed in detail in chapter 7.
‡Sitchin tells us that Enki had six sons, but one is not mentioned because scholars are not in agreement as to who he was.

mother he was dismayed at not having a wife and children, and that he had taken a liking to the earthling daughter of a high priest, an accomplished musician.[27] With his parent's permission, he married her. This couple produced a son, EN.SAG, which means "Lofty Lord." Although he was a demigod,* somehow this offspring was included on the list of Sumerians called gods. He was, in Sitchin's words, "the first demigod who was [considered] a god."[28] Later, after a military feat in which he was successful, he was given the name Nabu.

It is important to remember that Enlil had made it clear at the time before the Deluge that intermarriage of gods with earthlings was unacceptable; in fact he felt it was morally reprehensible. Marduk's intermarriage certainly must have contributed to Enlil's angst because by forging this union, as a member of the royal family, he set a precedent that would serve as a bad example for other Anunnaki. It is interesting that Enki approved of this relationship, an action that may also have contributed to the Enki-Enlil clan animosity.

Marduk rose to prominence in Egypt, where Sitchin surmises he was seen as the Egyptian god Ra. Egypt was Enki's domain, so, Marduk's power there is understandable. However, that was not enough for Marduk. The information Sitchin gathered points to Marduk's almost uncontrollable ambition to gain control over Earth. If Enki, his farther, had not lost his pre-eminent place as Earth's leader, Marduk would have inherited that role legally. His behavior tells us he believed he still was entitled to that birthright.

Marduk's infamy as a troublemaker further stems from several events, but the most prominent one records the accusation against him of murder. He was found to be either closely associ-

---

*A demigod was considered one-third mortal and two-thirds a god.

ated with, or the perpetrator of, the murder of Dumuzi, Ishtar's husband and Enki's youngest son. Inanna/Ishtar accused Marduk of this crime, and wanted him executed. But Anu intervened, and suggested Marduk instead be tried in the courts. Ishtar did not wait for the legal judgment; she went after Marduk herself, chasing him deep into the Great Pyramid and yelled her threats into this structure. But Marduk did not respond. A cylinder seal depicts Inanna's confrontation, showing her in her familiar half-naked pose, standing near the pyramids of Giza (see figure 2.1).

Ishtar was ready to use her own weapons to attack him there, but Anu interceded again, telling her that if she fired into the Pyramid, Marduk might use the weapon built into that structure to defend himself.* This episode substantiated Sitchin's contention that the Great Pyramid was a weapon. Subsequent research has shown this to be the case.

A longstanding argument of the Egyptians is that they built the Great Pyramid in historic times, and that it was built as a pharaoh's tomb. The Sumerian tablet records gave Sitchin the ammunition to dispute that claim. However, the Egyptians do not accept the ancient evidence, and in fact gave Sitchin a hard time when he wanted to visit that country. The Egyptians do not want to even hear of any information that would contradict their belief that the Great Pyramid was built by Egyptians for Egyptian burial purposes.

With her resolve to see Marduk dead, Ishtar made sure he

---

*This ancient record of the pyramid as a weapon is confirmed by a modern scientific finding that supports the idea that the Great Pyramid was a "paleo-ancient weapon." Described in scientific language as a "conjugate mirror and howitzer" or "coupled harmonic oscillator" in the research of the modern physicist Joseph P. Farrell, this idea is discussed in depth in his 2001 book *The Giza Death Star*.

Fig. 2.1. Cylinder seal pictogram: Inanna/Ishtar
shown in her familiar enticing half-naked pose.

was imprisoned by sealing him inside the pyramid with no way
to escape. Her intent was to deprive him of food and water,
and thus kill him by passive means. Sitchin tells us that the
tablet describing this event was found in numerous fragments.
However, because of the work of the Sumerian scholar, Samuel
Noah Kramer, we now have these words and from them we learn
of Marduk's fate as planned by Inanna/Ishtar:

> *In a great envelope that is sealed,*
> *With no one to offer him nourishment;*
> *Alone to suffer,*
> *The potable water source to be cut off.* [29]

Just before Marduk starved to death, Anunnaki experts
entered the pyramid and freed him. The words Sitchin quoted
from the ancient text to explain what the rescuers did (with their
special tools that could bore through limestone and other stone

blocks), are from a tablet he does not identify, but he writes that these rescuers: "hollowing into its insides they shall twistingly bore."[30] Sitchin offers us an historically extraordinary explanation, telling us that only the Anunnaki who had the pyramid's plan in hand could have known the interior design and how to bore through built-in obstructions to access the Grand Gallery where Marduk was held. Thus, Sitchin is telling us *who built the Great Pyramid*. Sitchin's knowledge of the pyramid's interior structures is cited as impressive and authentic by a modern author, Joseph P. Farrell, a scholar who published a thorough study of the ancient Great Pyramid in the first decade of the twenty-first century.[31]

After he was freed and stood trial, Marduk brought out evidence in the trial that was able to raise sufficient doubt as to whether Dumuzi died by accident or at his hand. Although he was exonerated, Marduk was forced into exile. He lived in seclusion in Egypt under the name "Amen, the Hidden One." When he emerged from that banishment, he petitioned to return to Sumer, and when he finally did return, he took control of the city of Babylon by trickery, proclaiming himself supreme leader of Babylon (and therefore Sumer). He also boasted that he would capture and control the Anunnaki spaceport in the central Sinai. This was seen as a serious threat against all the Nefilim and Anunnaki as the spaceport located there after the Deluge was the strategic lifeline between Nibiru and Earth.

Marduk's braggadocio was seen by Enki's other son, Nergal, and Enlil's son, Ninurta, as a really serious threat that must be stopped at all cost. After Nergal pleaded unsuccessfully with his father Enki to take serious action to stop Marduk, these two Nefilim offspring joined forces and devised a plan that received the approval of Anu and the Nefilim council. Their plan to stop

Marduk and his son, Nabu, from gaining access to the sacred Sinai spaceport site was of monumental importance to Earth's history because it involved the use of Anunnaki nuclear weapons.

Nergal and Ninurta unleashed these ultimate weapons—nuclear devices previously brought from Nibiru—that had been stored underground somewhere in southern Africa. After carefully targeted detonations sites were identified, designed to stay within approved target sites in Sinai, both the spaceport and its control center were totally destroyed. (For the full story of the use of nuclear weapons, see chapter 7 of this book.) These actions created a fallout cloud that caused the demise of Sumer; every living thing inside the blast zone and in the path of the nuclear cloud was extinguished. (See appendix B for Sitchin's discussion of this catastrophe.) The year of this nuclear holocaust was 2024 BCE.

Enlil's Son, Ninurta

Enlil's son and rightful heir, NIN.UR.TA (born by his sister Ninhursag) was also known as "Lord Who Completes the Foundation." He was a heroic being, who "went forth with net and rays of light" to battle an enemy for his father.[32] Sitchin tells us that ancient portraits show him holding a weapon that could shoot "bolts of light," presumably a laser weapon. However, Ninurta's greatest victory was altruistic, as he championed the leadership of the "gods" on Earth. It was a battle with a character known as Zu, who was Nefilim, but was deemed to be evil. This saga is told in Sitchin's book, *The 12th Planet*.[33] We will summarize it here.

Though of questionable background, Zu found his way into the good graces of one of the Igigi, those astronauts who manned the spacecraft that circled and monitored Earth from above.

Plate 1. Zecharia Sitchin at Hagar Qim (ancient site),
a major temple on Malta.
(Photograph by author)

Plate 2. Avebury stone, southern England.
(Photograph by author)

Plate 3. The author next to an Avebury stone.

Plate 4. Pentre Ifan Dolmen, Wales. The caprock is supported by two upright stones on the thick end and one on the thin end.

Plate 5. Earth Chronicles Expedition group at Stonehenge.
(Photograph courtesy of Zecharia Sitchin, *Journeys to the Mythical Past*)

Plate 6. Replica of Anunnaki birth mother—
chosen to increase the human population.
(Photograph by author)

Plate 7. Landscape view of the sacred Delphi Temple of Apollo; photo taken on Sitchin tour.
(Photograph by author)

Plate 8. Qumran wadi with cave and eroded end of plateau where settlement ruins are found; photo taken on Sitchin tour. (Photograph by author)

Plate 9. Qumran caves where Dead Sea scrolls were found; photo taken on a Sitchin tour. (Photograph by author)

Plate 10. Qumran ruins on the shore of Dead Sea; photo taken on a Sitchin tour. (Photograph by author)

Plate 11. Ritual bath inside the ruins at Qumran;
photo taken on Sitchin tour. (Photograph by author)

Plate 12. The colossal Trilithon in the massive western retaining wall, Baalbek. (Photograph courtesy of Zecharia Sitchin, *The Earth Chronicles Expeditions*)

Plate 13. The immense stone block in the quarry, Baalbek.
(Photograph courtesy of Zecharia Sitchin, *The Earth Chronicles Expeditions*)

Plate 14. Zecharia Sitchin leading a tour in Mexico.
(Photograph by Wally Motloch)

Plate 15. Sitchin leading a tour at the ancient structure
at Dzibilchaltún, the oldest site on the Yucatán.
(Photograph by author)

Plate 16. Zecharia Sitchin and his beloved wife, Rina, on one of the Sitchin tours. (Photograph by author)

When that group had a complaint against Enlil, Zu was sent to negotiate with him. With evil intentions foremost in his mind, Zu was able to convincingly indicate he could be trusted and was given access to the mission control center, that vital site that was under Enlil's control and that held the technology that linked Earth with Nibiru. Zu took advantage of Enlil's trust by using trickery and lies and stole the sacred tablets that controlled the ability of Earth to communicate with Nibiru. He then fled in a stolen spacecraft and flew to the "Mountain of the Sky-Chamber," where he disabled the stolen technology.

When Anu was told of Zu's theft, he made it clear that Zu must be captured. At first none of the Nefilim stepped up to undertake that dangerous mission. However, then Enlil's legal heir, Ninurta, came forward. His mother armed him with a "weapon of Brilliance." With her assistance, technology referred to as "whirlwinds" created a dust storm that provided cover for a battle that ensued. After many powerful weapons were put to use, Zu was subdued and captured, then brought to Enlil, who convened the Seven Great Anunnaki to conduct a trial. Zu was found guilty and sentenced to death. Ninurta, his vanquisher, cut his throat. Sitchin shows a cylinder seal of Zu dressed as a bird (with a feathered suit) that recorded the death of Zu for posterity (and for our edification).[34]

On a more positive note, Ninurta undertook to make the water-soaked uplands of Sumer functional following the Deluge. Sitchin tells us that "Ninurta rushed from place to place in the mountains in his airship," managing project after project to control the water-soaked lands. But his flying vehicle crashed on a mountain summit. Ninurta survived that event, and he continued his efforts to return Sumer to a productive region again. He is credited as the one who brought agriculture back to humankind.

Enki's Son, Dumuzi

Dumuzi was the youngest but also a notable son of Enki, but not for involvement in wars or flood control, or any other strategic accomplishments. He was the intended bridegroom of Ishtar (also called Inanna), Enki's granddaughter and one of the most notoriously important offspring in the Nefilim dynasty. Much of the story involving Dumuzi's love for this flamboyant goddess is told in the chapter focused on Anunnaki love and lovemaking (chapter 4), so we will not repeat it here. Suffice it to say, Dumuzi and Ishtar were married, but produced no children. They were separated by their powerful parental clans, Dumuzi was killed, and Inanna went on to live a notable life. Sitchin likens this saga to that of Shakespeare's *Romeo and Juliet*, calling both this tale and the one designed by Shakespeare very sad stories. We do not profile Ishtar here, as we give her story ample attention in chapter 4.

Gods, Planets, and God

What is interesting, but lends confusion to Sumerian scholarship, is that in a translation of a classic Sumerian creation epic, the word *god* is used in that epic to designate the planets. The *Enuma Elish* tells us that a planetary body that was spun off from the Sun in the formative phases of our solar system was called a "god." Sitchin devoted considerable time to the study of this very important set of tablets. A quote from the original text illustrates the way the word *god* is used, and illuminates some other important points:

> *When in the heights Heaven has not been named,*
> *And below, Earth had not been called,*
> *Naught, but primordial APSU, their Begetter,*
> *MUMMU, and TIAMAT—she who bore them all,*
> *Their waters were mingled together.*
> *No reed had yet formed, no marshland had*
>   *appeared,*
> *None of the gods had yet been brought into being.*
> *None bore a name, their destinies were*
>   *undetermined,*
> *Then it was that gods were formed in their midst.*[35]

We suspect that even the original translators of this epic did not fully understand what "Nefilim" meant when they read the tablet clay materials on which this story was laid out. This translation refers to the planets as *gods* and gave them gender designations. Behaviors also were ascribed to the planetary entities. In this excerpt of the much longer text, Apsu is the sun, assigned a female gender; Mummu was later known as Mercury; Tiamat (also labeled female) was the name of the planetary body that was *smashed* and moved to become planet Earth. "Destinies" were the rotational paths of the planetary bodies. The reference to "waters" indicates formative basic life-giving elements (material) floating about in space.

This multi-tablet story, in reality, is a lesson in celestial mechanics and introduces us to the role of electromagnetism as a force, acting along with gravity, to generate interactions between celestial (planetary) bodies. This scientific knowledge was well understood in Nefilim culture. One of Sitchin's most interesting revelations—one that no doubt caused a "eureka" moment in his thinking—came as he studied the *Enuma Elish*. When Sitchin substituted the word *planets* for *gods*, a very different perception filled his thinking. Enormous clarity must have invaded his thoughts and opened his consideration for the possibilities that other misinterpretations might be hidden in the redacted materials with which he worked.

An interesting set of beliefs, implying rejection of historical reality that the "ancient ones" actually existed, came forward when monotheism entered the world's religious thought. This belief introduced the concept of "one supreme being" that humans should pray to and call on. Ancient history carried the concept of multiple "gods" down through the ages, but somewhere along the way it was deemed unacceptable to continue the belief in many gods. A one-God concept became prayerful practice and entered the central belief structure of Jewish, Christian, and Islamic religions.*

It seems to be a basic human desire to have an "object of belief," a supreme being, an ethereal focus that functions as an unseen and powerful force interested enough in devout human individuals that this force is ready to provide assistance. No doubt there *is* such an unseen supportive power available to humans, but one must conceptualize it in order to use it.†

---

*Wikipedia offers this information: *Monotheism* characterizes the traditions including (but not limited to) the Bahá'í Faith, Christianity, Sikhism, Islam, Judaism, Rastafarianism, Vaishnavism, and Zoroastrianism. Elements of the one-god belief are discernible in numerous other religions.

†An informative source supporting this statement can be found in Frank DeMarco's *The Cosmic Internet* (2011). He refers to entities on the "other side of the veil," which he calls "the guys upstairs." These unseen beings can be contacted in meditative prayer and provide advice and perspectives for us to consider.

Most modern believers in a one-God concept do not even want to consider a historically derived alternative identification of their deity. What is important is that many believers—especially Christians and Jews—conceptualize God as a man. This idea has its truth in Judaic literature. Sitchin tells us: "The God of the ancient Hebrews could be seen face-to-face, could be wrestled with, could be heard and spoken to; he had a head and feet, hands and fingers, and a waist."[36] The original "gods" of olden times, especially Enki and Enlil, generated a historical record that impressed their presence into ancient cultural history; perhaps, in a misunderstood way, they gave rise to notions of multiple gods. Is it possible that biblical history compressed (for whatever theological and/or political reasons) these two individuals into one to accomplish the goals of monotheism?

Within theological circles, a debate exists as to whether God is *merciful* or *vengeful*. The answer to this query depends on whether the discussion focuses on the Nefilim information given to us by Sitchin, or refers to an even higher deity, the *God of the Universe* (such as, perhaps, the God revered by the Nefilim). If we use Sitchin's information, there were two Nefilim leaders, each called a god in the tablet sources. They each viewed humans differently. Enki was the *merciful* one who strived to save earthlings at the time the flood occurred because he understood the value of humans as workers, and he was instrumental in creating them. He figured out how to allow one small family to survive the Deluge, so we can conclude that he held a benevolent feeling toward some humans.

The opposing view, as it was revealed by Enlil's behavior (and statements), was filled with hostility and intolerance toward humans. He was the *vengeful* "god," forcing all the Nefilim to pledge not to tell earthlings about the coming Deluge and allowing that disaster to "take them off the face of the Earth." Enlil clearly stated that he wanted humans to be eradicated, mostly because of their immoral behaviors. According to the texts, Enlil actually wanted to see that all those "bothersome, noisy, gluttonous, immoral" earthlings become victims of the flood.[37] These views held by Enlil indeed were vengeful.

Sitchin's work forces us to at least contemplate the idea that some creative rethinking, or perhaps a simplification of the God-concept, has taken place in the course of religious history. We do not know how long after the Nefilim were on Earth that the little "g" was changed to the capital letter "G," but likely it has changed our understanding of how Enki and Enlil are viewed historically. The reality is that two became one. We perhaps need to rethink modern religious understandings in light of the very ancient historical material Sitchin brings to our attention.

To be aware that what we are told in religious teachings perhaps is not the "end of the story," but instead is an explanation we have been taught that perhaps needs to be examined more critically, may be uncomfortable—if not abhorrent—to some. If our supposition is true, that this "merger" happened in the course of the unfolding of religious history, it is not a threat to any modern belief system to entertain an alternative explanation; it merely is an important clarification we could (should) consider.

3

The Creation of Earthlings

Don't become a mere recorder of facts,
but try to penetrate the mystery
of their origin.

IVAN PAVLOV

How did humans come to live on Earth? This question is challenging, wrapped as it is in debate. It also is as exciting a question as it is captivating. This query's wording presumes that a human species lived elsewhere in the universe and someone or something brought humanoid life here. Could that be possible? Or are there other explanations to be found for human existence on planet Earth?

While Zecharia Sitchin does *not* entertain this question in just the way we posed it, his research into the ancient clay tablets writings does tell us "All the Sumerian texts assert that the gods created Man."[1] Also the biblical evidence indicates that man was not a god nor was he created in the heavens. It was clear that while humans lacked the godly characteristics of "knowing" and "longevity," they were "in all other respects created in the image (*selem*) and likeness (*dmut*) of [their] Creator(s). The use of both terms in the text was meant to leave no doubt that Man was similar to the God(s) both physically and emotionally, externally and internally."[2]

These comments are very enlightening. Sitchin goes on to wonder "how could a new creature possibly be a virtual physical, mental, and emotional replica of the Nefilim? How, indeed, was Man created?"[3] Obviously, Sitchin penetrated the mysteries, and was not just a recorder of facts, as Pavlov suggested. We will follow a fact-focused exploration into Sitchin's research to see where it leads and what we can learn about this fascinating topic. Sitchin, a determined researcher, did just that—followed the facts—when his study of the ancient Sumerian tablets led him to the topic of the *creation of humans*.

The Debate about Human Origins

Undoubtedly, knowing the origins of the human species that now populates planet Earth is important. This topic has been long studied by physical anthropologists, genetic scientists, and others curious about this issue. The discussion of the origin of the human species has prompted heated disputes. We will attempt to unwrap this contentious debate here. Essentially this discussion asks: Did the God of the Bible "create" humans from some substance found on Earth? Or did the forces of nature work a progressive developmental change on a primeval creature who, very slowly, underwent genetic change by processes called *mutation* and *natural selection*, as put forward in the writings of the English naturalist, Charles Darwin?

While evolutionary scientists may believe that human genetic change has been occurring across the thousands of millennia of life on Earth, evidence to lock down this explanation of how progress (or change) occurs in humans is scarce.* Would such slow changes lead to today's intelligent humans? Even if one looked for cognitive change beginning with Stone Age man (six hundred thousand or even fewer years ago), it is doubtful that evolutionary change would provide unambiguous evidence that would result in today's intellectually capable and creative humans.† There just has not been sufficient time for the types of change that differentiate primitive beings (Neanderthal) from the modern (Cro-Magnon) human species—*Homo sapiens sapiens*—to have occurred.[4]

If Darwin's explanation is not realistic, what other source can be used to document the origin of modern humans? Is it possible there is another answer to how modern intelligent humans came into existence? Sitchin's research tells us that the answer to that question is "yes." According to him there is biblical and anthropological evidence to support a different explanation. In his characteristic way, Sitchin followed his inclination to find answers to clues contained in the ancient clay tablets records; he was able to

---

*According to Robert A. Guisepi in his article "Prehistoric Cultural Stage, or Level of Human Development, Characterized by the Creation and Use of Stone Tools" (on the International World History website, http://history-world.org/stone_age.htm), dates for the start of what is known as the Stone age vary, but some sources give the time of origin at six hundred thousand years ago, with an end about eight thousand years ago with the appearance of pottery and metalwork.

†The following website provides scholarly evidence for understanding the lives of early humans, information drawn from the Smithsonian Institution's Human Origins Program, "Human Characteristics: Social Life," http://humanorigins.si.edu/human-characteristics/social.

penetrate the tablet language to uncover evidence documenting that *Homo sapiens* developed by genetic manipulation carried out by the Nefilim.

The Sitchin Evidence of Human Creation

Sitchin tells us that the evidence clearly indicates that *deliberate genetic modification* explains the appearance of modern intellectual humans on Earth. He weighs in as a critic of the sweeping implications of the Darwinian explanations, and his message helps us see the flaws in the reasoning that points to a slow developmental trajectory.

> Evolution can explain the general course of events that caused life and life's forms to develop on Earth from the simplest one-celled creature to Man. But evolution cannot account for the appearance of *Homo sapiens*, which happened virtually overnight in terms of the millions of years evolution requires, and with no evidence of earlier stages that would indicate a gradual change from *Homo erectus*.[5]

The tablet evidence clearly indicates that *Homo sapiens* was a result of genetic manipulation by a scientific team from the space traveler group who came down to Earth and worked out the details of this design project some three hundred thousand years ago. As mentioned earlier, we humans are here on Earth because the Nefilim needed our kind (intelligent willing workers) to rectify a labor shortage at their gold mines. Whereas some hold the view that early humans were created to worship their creators, Sitchin points out that "the term commonly translated as 'worship' was in fact *avod* ('work')."[6] He amplifies the role of the first humans with this statement: "Ancient and biblical Man did *not* "worship" his god; *he worked for him*" (emphasis added).[7]

The following excerpt is spoken by the leader of those space travelers:

> *I will produce a lowly Primitive;*
> *"Man" shall be his name.*
> *I will create a Primitive Worker;*
> *He will be charged with service of the gods,*
> *That they might have their ease.*[8]

Importantly, the two Nefilim scientists—Enki and Ninhursag—did not develop the human being out of nothing. Sitchin's words here give us the most profound statement we find in any of his several books, and they will serve as a beacon to guide our inquiry deeper into this topic. He makes it clear that the human "origins debate" is not an either-or issue, but derives, in actuality, from *both* explanations.* Sitchin states:

> Man is the product of evolution; but modern Man, *Homo sapiens*, is the product of the "gods." For, some time circa 300,000 years ago, the Nefilim took ape-man (*Homo erectus*) and implanted on him their own image and likeness.[9]

In plain words, humans evolved *and* were created. A partially evolved being was used as the raw material, and genes from an

---

*For a more extensive discussion of the origins debate see my earlier book, *The Legacy of Zecharia Sitchin*: 90–93.

Fig. 3.1. Tablet depicting Enki (center) and Ninhursag in a laboratory creating the "perfect" being.

Anunnaki were added to create the "perfect" being. Enki and Ninhursag did this through using their knowledge of genetic engineering.

Sitchin describes Nefilim ingenuity:

When [the leadership council] said to him, "How will you create such a thing?" Enki, their leader, said that, and this is a quote from the text, *"This being already exists. All that we have to do is put our mark on it."* Then the text, in great detail, described the process that the only modern parallel to it is that of bringing about test-tube babies. They mixed the genes of one of their young males with the egg of an ape woman . . . and after mixing the two, re-implanted fertilized eggs in the wombs of some of their own females.

Now, some biologists and other experts in fertility tell me that this little detail [works]. The fact that I quoted it from the [ancient] text, that the fertilized eggs of the ape woman were re-implanted in the wombs of females who arrived on earth, let's say the ancient astronaut females, has great significance to the nature of the being that was finally created; that is very important. . . . We are *Homo sapiens*, not the hominid race which appeared on earth through evolution.[10]

In an effort to underscore this information about the availability of a humanoid who was an existing source of usable genes for the creation of humans, we will use Sitchin's exact words:

> During a celestial collision, their planet [meaning Nibiru] had seeded Earth with its life. Therefore this being that was available [to Enki] was really akin to the Nefilim—though in a less evolved form.
>
> A gradual process of domestication through generations of breeding and selection would not do [to solve the labor problem]. What was needed was a quick process, one that would permit "mass production" of the new workers . . . [and] the answer [was] to "imprint" the image of the gods on the being that already existed.[11]

The existing hominid, the "underdeveloped" one, was at an early stage of evolutionary improvement, but held a degree of intelligence that could be raised when the "image and likeness" of the gods was inserted into its genetic structure. Because of this topic's importance to us, Sitchin devoted an entire chapter in his first book to the information explaining this episode, titling it "The Creation of Man." Sitchin states that:

"The Adam" of the Bible was not the genus *Homo,* but the being who is our ancestor—the first *Homo sapiens.* It is modern Man as we know him that the Nefilim created. . . . Enki [was] informed that the gods had decided to form an *adamu,* and that it was his task to find the means. He replied:

"The creature whose name you uttered—

IT EXISTS!"[12]

This hominid walked about, drinking on hands and knees from streams and engaging in sexual acts with animals. In fact, one of those "ape men" was selected by a Nefilim goddess, Ninsun, to be "tamed" so he could become a companion to her troublesome son, Gilgamesh. His story is related in the *Epic of Gilgamesh,* which is considered to be the world's oldest piece of literature. Gilgamesh had been born of Ninsun's marital union with a human who was a priest in the ancient city of Erech. This allowed him to consider himself two-thirds a god by Anunnaki tradition. Enkidu, Gilgamesh's hairy naked companion-to-be, was a "kind of Stone Age man" (Sitchin's words). He was raised up from his "animal-oriented" ways to be a companion to Gilgamesh by being carefully taught by an Anunnaki woman of "service." Her lessons were focused on his sexual behaviors with women so that he would be *unacceptable* to animals, thus considered civilized.*

The primitive worker, *Homo sapiens,* who was crafted some three hundred thousand years ago jump-started the process that continued and eventually resulted in the creation of humans (*Homo sapiens sapiens*) as we know them—in other words *us.*

---

*The full story of Gilgamesh and Enkidu appears in Sitchin's book, *The 12th Planet,* and now also under a separate cover in the form of a novel, published posthumously in 2013 by Sitchin's grandson as his final book.

That earthlings were valuable to the Nefilim is confirmed by a story relating what took place when Enlil was banished from Sumer because of a moral transgression. He was forced to go to the site of the mining activity in southern Africa, where he observed the "willing workers" in action. He realized the value of these primitive workers and decided to take some of them back to Sumer to be the servants (not slaves) of the Nefilim. In making this decision, Enlil clashed mightily with Enki and launched an armed attack against the Land of the Mines.[13] Animosity between these two half-brothers had a long history, and this action on Enlil's part was just one more episode. Enlil was successful in taking some of the workers to the settlements in Sumer. Soon thereafter, the willing and intelligent workers became extremely valuable to the Nefilim as scribes. Because of the intelligence of those scribes we have the artifacts that bring us these valuable and important bodies of explanation.

The Implementation of the Creation Process

The next step in the creation of the primitive workers required the enlistment of a cadre of Anunnaki women to become *birth mothers*—seven to produce males and seven to produce females. This step explains how Enki could get the workforce needed to solve the manpower problem within a reasonably short time. (See the replica of Anunnaki birth mother in the color insert, plate 6.)

In a real sense, Earth's population would do well to be indebted to Enki, the chief scientist of the Nefilim, for the creative effort he used that brought *us* into existence.* We have

---

*Another way to think about the consequences of human procreation is that it has led to overpopulation that is threatening Earth's capacity to feed the huge human population that has resulted.

evidence for this valuable explanation of how humankind came into existence due to Sitchin's willingness to probe deeply into the ancient clay tablet records. The necessary aspects of these genetic science procedures now are in modern use and are valuable bodies of information to aid our understanding of ancient history. This is just one more example in support of Sitchin's proclamation that modern science *finally* is catching up with ancient knowledge. '

Drawing on another ancient Sumerian source, one that was used by writers (or editors) of the Bible when the Book of Genesis was adapted from Sumerian sources, we read this statement, which Sitchin calls "astonishing":

> *And Elohim said:*
> *"Let us make Man in our image,*
> *after our likeness."*[14]

These ancient sources affirm that we, "the earthlings," as the space travelers called our species, were made to look like those who created us. Tablet pictograms document this. But what about the phrase "after our likeness"? Here are the tablet verses that will help us to understand:

> *In the clay, god and Man shall be bound,*
> *to a unity brought together;*
> *So that to the end of days*
> *the Flesh and the Soul*
> *which in a god have ripened—*
> *that Soul in a blood-kinship be bound;*
> *As its Sign life shall proclaim.*

So that this not be forgotten
Let the "Soul" in a blood-kinship be bound.[15]

Here is the "in the image and after the likeness" explanation. Enki did indeed make humans like the gods. Sitchin's words again carry a profound meaning for us:

These are strong words, little understood by scholars. The text states that the god's blood was mixed into the clay so as to bind god and Man genetically "to the end of days" so that both flesh ("image") and the soul ("likeness") of the gods would become imprinted upon Man in a kinship of blood that could never be severed.[16]

The "clay" was an analogy for the building block of the genetic process (unlike in the Bible where it is taken literally to mean a type of dirt). Sitchin's words unravel for us the complex understanding of what the mixing of the "blood" of a god into the "clay" means:

The "divine" element required was not simply the dripping blood of a god, but something more basic and lasting. The god that was selected . . . had TE.E.MA, a term the leading authorities on the text . . . translate as "personality." But, the ancient term is much more specific; it literally means "that which houses that which binds the memory."[17]

In an Akkadian text, another version of this same term can be found as *etemu,* translated as "spirit." The implication that Sitchin drew was that something else was the repository of human individuality. He surmises that the scientific process Enki used "refined" the actual blood until the DNA used in the genetic impress was like that of the gods. The altered DNA was all that remained.

If one believes that the soul shapes behavior, then we humans behave in similar ways to the Nefilim gods, our creators, who came down to live on Earth many hundreds of thousands of years ago. We are intelligent, capable, and inventive—like the gods of olden times.

The Knowledge of Adam and Eve

When we probe even further, we learn something more interesting about the well-known biblical story of the Garden of Eden. The Bible tells us that two of these "willing workers," a male and a female, were assigned by Enlil to a tree garden in the E.DIN. They were told to take special care of two trees that were extremely valuable to the Nefilim and Anunnaki. Enlil gave the female, Eve, a specific order: he told her not to touch (probably meaning "not to eat") the fruit of the Tree of Knowing.

These two earthlings, Adam and Eve, were put to work in the orchard without any awareness that their creator, Enki, had genetically programmed them to be like the Nefilim in that they, too, could procreate. Enlil knew they held this capability, and decided to keep it from them. The couple continued to work naked, like all the other created workers. Whether for spite against Enlil or personal motivations, Enki decided to visit Eve in the garden, and there he urged her to partake of the fruit of the Tree of Knowing. This meant she had to deliberately disobey her master, Enlil, who had forbidden her to touch the fruit from that tree. Enki probably had decided that this couple should be told that they had the same procreative capability as the Anunnaki, so he took an action that, in essence, double-crossed his brother. Enki first informed Eve to eat that "forbidden fruit," and she then shared her newly acquired permission with Adam. She gave him some of that fruit to eat.

What Enki did was merely to urge the female to eat a fruit that likely was an aphrodisiac growing on that special tree, the Tree of Knowing. When she consumed the fruit, she "knew"— physiologically, she "knew." She told her partner, he ate, and his body responded as well. After eating they both knew they had sexual (meaning procreative) capability. This awareness also brought them to realize their nakedness. The "gods" were clothed, but Adam and Eve had been roaming about, tending the garden naked, and did not even recognize this difference. However, as soon as Enlil saw they had "covered their naked-ness," he understood what had happened. Here is the text, now unpacked for us to better understand Enlil's discovery of their transgression.

> *And they heard the sound of the Deity Yahweh*
> *Walking in the orchard in the day's breeze,*
> *And the Adam and his mate hid*
> *from the Deity Yahweh amongst the orchard's trees.*
> *And the Deity Yahweh called to the Adam*
> *And said: "Where are thou?"*
> *And he answered:*
> *"Thy sound I heard in the orchard*
> *and I was afraid, for I am naked;*
> *and I hid."*
> *And He [Yahweh] said:*
> *"Who told thee that thou are naked?*

> *Hast thou eaten of the tree,*
> *whereof I commanded thee not to eat?*"[18]

In essence, the couple had enjoyed innocence, and thereafter that quality of life was gone; sexual awareness ensued. It is interesting—and perplexing—that the texts refer to this knowing as the knowledge of good and evil. One can only wonder at the motivations behind Enki's action. He was known to be one who had a generous proclivity for sexual encounters. Did he want these humans to share those erotic feelings? Or did Enki just want to one-up his brother by urging the humans to go against Enlil's orders? Is it possible that Enki wanted humans to increase in numbers? We are not given tablet evidence that would allow us to go confidently beyond the information we already have brought forward.

Enlil, no doubt, had political reasons for why humans should remain ignorant of their procreation capability. Enki, on the other hand, perhaps as an act of spitefulness against Enlil's command power, felt differently. We will never know the motivations behind the actions of these two brothers, but what we *do* know is that human sexual awareness made its debut for humans in that garden in the lands the ancients called E.DIN.

This story is well known, but not with Enki playing a role. Rather it is his *symbol* that is referred to as the informant. Enki's symbol was the *snake*, stemming from their plentiful supply in the swampy place where he built his first house. Enki's symbol was depicted graphically as two entwined snakes. This symbol is familiar to us as the *caduceus*, the symbol of the medical profession. This symbol's association with the way humans were given knowledge of their sexual capabilities is unfortunate, but perhaps the original redactors preferred to assign a lowly snake (rather than a Nefilim god) to this provocative role. Human sexual procreative capability owes a debt to Enki. He made sure that the created humans were akin to the gods in every physiological as well as intellectual way.

The Implications of Human Procreativity

The consequence of Adam and Eve having acquired "knowing" was expulsion from the Garden of Eden. Enlil is reported to have been afraid that these earthlings might also eat from the other special tree, the Tree of Life, the one that would allow them to escape mortality. Tasting *that* fruit would have given these humans both of the primary differences setting the "gods" apart—procreative ability and longevity. What he did to prevent this from ever occurring was to remove the couple from not only the temptation, but from the possibility of another revelation by Enki. A Sumerian text provides valuable enlightenment to what was behind Enlil's seemingly vengeful decision:

> *Then did the Deity Yahweh say:*
> *"Behold, the Adam has become as one of us,*
> *to know good and evil.*
> *And now might he not put forth his hand*
> *And partake also of the Tree of Life,*
> *And eat, and live forever?"*
> *And the Deity Yahwah expelled the Adam*
> *From the orchard of Eden.*[19]

This event has come to be called, by biblical scholars, the "fall of mankind." Enlil did not just transfer Adam and Eve to another less tempting location, but banished them from Eden completely. He sent them to the Abzu, the designation for the African region where the gold mining operation was located.

What followed was Enlil's announcement of Eve's punishment for sharing this sexual information with Adam. He told her that thereafter, as she used her new procreative capability and bore children, she would suffer painful childbirth. No doubt the punishment was given to Eve because she was the one who convinced Adam to eat the forbidden fruit. Eve was given what some would say is the bane of womanhood—the labor pains of childbirth.

> *And to the woman He said:*
> *"I will greatly multiply thy suffering*
> *by thy pregnancy.*
> *In suffering shalt thou bear children,*
> *yet to thy mate shall be thy desire"* . . .
> *And the Adam named his wife "Eve,"*
> *For she was the mother of all who lived.*[20]

Sitchin tells us that the acquisition of the sexual knowledge given for the primary purpose of procreation was a crucial step in the development of humans. However, Sitchin tells us that even lacking sexual "knowing" and the knowledge of the longevity of the gods, the Adam was "similar to the God(s) both physically and emotionally, externally and internally."[21]

"Godlike" Workers, Not Slaves!

There are writers who seem to believe that humans were created to be subservient, in other words, to be slaves. Even though the slave phenomenon was prevalent early in human history (and has continued in some places around the globe even today), the view that humans were created to be slaves falls by the wayside as we look at the evidence. Slavery is the antithesis of intelligent development. Slavery is a reprehensible (perhaps even a demonic) force that some humans use to exert ultimate power and control over other human beings. It is important to emphasize, according to the tablet evidence, that humans were *not* created as slaves. There is too much evidence to counter this twisted and erroneous interpretation. Those authors who espouse this negative interpretation of the creative evidence should re-read Sitchin, as it is contrary to his explanations.

To those who have set out this mistaken idea that humans were created to be slaves, and those who read and accept that interpretation, we offer the following clarification. It is the "masters" who dominate slaves. Slaves have no freedom of choice and are constrained by authority to do only the bidding of those authorities. For the most part, slaves have no freedom of movement, as in the ability to explore territory. Even the hunter-gatherer humans used their free will to make decisions. In the Bible story of the events in the Garden of Eden, Eve used her free will to inform Adam. Hunter-gatherers engaged in creative thinking in the development of tools and methods of successful hunting. While most early humans used their freedom for personal benefit and the benefit of those close to them, others might have been constrained by survival circumstances to live with group-imposed constraints on their personal freedom in order to survive. Even that was a choice, not an eventuality imposed by a master.

The history of human creativity and the movement decisions humans have undertaken throughout history are convincing evidence against the derogatory interpretation of the creative intention of the Nefilim as being slaves. And, we can see clear indications that humans are continuing to evolve, mostly through the creative technologies invented in the physical and cognitive sciences. The future holds even more promise of such developments as smart chips embedded into humans to enhance physical capability, and ideas that control physical technology are in more widespread use.* Already prostheses with neuroelectric capabilities assist amputees to regain close to normal function. Bioengineering possibilities seem almost limitless regarding further improvement of human capabilities. The inventive effort to give computers the decision-making capability to "think like humans" (called artificial intelligence) has been underway for years.

Are these increased capabilities usurping the role of a "creator," or is scientific knowledge of humans nudging the most intelligent among humankind to further the work of the "gods"? We probably never will know the answer to this question, but we do know that capabilities were "implanted" in humans by those who came down, and the process of human development has not yet reached its highest level of creativity.

In the next chapter we will explore a most interesting topic: the intimate interpersonal behavior of the Anunnaki. That they exhibited interpersonal attraction leading to sexual behavior percolates throughout Sitchin's discussions. Obviously, he felt that those behaviors that the space travelers brought with them from Nibiru (derived no doubt from typical behaviors they were accustomed to engaging in on their home planet) were an important aspect of their lives—and of ours.

---

*Here we refer to a new and emerging technology known as Google Glass.

4

Anunnaki Love
and Lovemaking

Love is of all passions the strongest,
for it attacks simultaneously
the head, the heart,
and the senses.

LAO-TZU

There are four pillars of love, namely,
psychological (mind), emotional (heart),
physical (body), and spiritual (spirit).
Without these pillars,
to feel love is at one's risk.

RAVINDRAN KRISHAN

*L*ove is an emotion known from very ancient times, according to the ancient clay tablet records. *Lovemaking* is the most prominent behavior discussed in the Sitchin treatment of the tablet stories related to this topic. Love as an interpersonal emotion is the motivation that characterizes several of the examples Sitchin highlights in his discussions, but there also are examples of actions associated with lust. Sometimes what seemed like lust initially was transformed into genuine love as a relationship developed.

When most modern humans think of love, those thoughts often encompass a complex set of behaviors exhibiting tender, caring feelings. In some contemporary literature love is dominated by feelings such as devotion, kindness, compassion, affection, an unselfish form of personal loyalty, and caring for another prompted by a benevolent concern for the good of that other person. Steadfast caring often dominates the behavioral pattern of both individuals who profess to be "in love."

On the other hand, the word *love* also can represent ardent attraction with an intense sexual goal. How do we know when genuine love is being displayed between two individuals? Identifying love-oriented behavior is much more difficult than identifying sexual attraction. Typically the love emotion is evidenced by interpersonal attachment, but it also must be distinguished from friendship. There are several examples of sexual attachments in Anunnaki stories.

Love may be associated with the intention or need to procreate, which frequently motivated Enki. Enki gave Adam and Eve procreation capability, but their story is devoid of any evidence of a love-oriented emotional attraction. In fact, procreation may have been the predominant reason Enki urged Eve to eat the forbidden fruit. Enki may only have wanted to see the earthlings continue as a species by using their physiological procreative capability.

Popular culture embraced the pervasiveness of the love emotion in 1958 when the idea of love as a global "engine" became a popular song. This song asserts that "Love Makes the World Go Round."*

---

*The most popular version of this song was recorded by Perry Como. He made two recordings in 1958, on September 5 and September 16. The single was released by RCA Victor Records.

That title now is a well-worn phrase and is appropriate to describe the "eros" focus of the royal Nefilim who first settled Earth. They frequently interspersed their leadership responsibilities with sexual behaviors. The evidence Sitchin found indicates how indispensable intimate sexual relationships were to them.

The tablets portray not only a dominant emotional need for sexual satisfaction, but perhaps a lifestyle proclivity of royal Nefilim, and we can assume they represent similar motivations for satisfaction of those needs felt by earthlings. Our discussion will point out a few examples of actual love, of caring and emotional attachment that continued through time. In one tablet record the word *love* is used to describe the emotions between two individuals—it involves Inanna and her intended husband, Dumuzi.

An array of sexually oriented behaviors may seem especially out-of-place topics to be given attention in books written by Sitchin. He was a stately, seemingly straight-laced gentleman, who always presented himself with a serious expression, a dignified demeanor, and a circumspect bearing. So, to find topics like seduction, lust, rape, and intercourse given attention in his works might seem out of character. However, it must be remembered that Sitchin held a strong commitment to accuracy and thoroughness in presenting his research findings. If the sources presented sexual material, Sitchin dealt with it in a straightforward and candid manner. Exploring the sexual behaviors of the Nefilim provides an insight into their personal proclivities as well as a key to understanding how sexual behavior was used to keep the dynasty's power within "proper" bloodlines. Sitchin also felt this material was part of the legitimate history of the Nefilim. In fact, he tells us this:

> The Mesopotamian texts speak freely and eloquently of sex and lovemaking among the gods. . . . There are texts describing tender love between gods and their consorts; illicit love between a maiden and her lover; and violent love (as when Enlil raped Ninlil). There is a profusion of texts describing lovemaking and actual intercourse among the gods—with their official consorts or unofficial concubines, with their sisters and daughters and even granddaughters; in fact making love to the latter was a favorite pastime engaged in by Enki.[1]

Sitchin always was true to his sources, and candidly tells us that intimate relationships were regarded by the Nefilim leadership as personally and perhaps even physiologically important. Just as in modern society, these behaviors were a significant part of Nefilim society, engaged in for several purposes, such as to achieve a political goal, for procreation, or for personal satisfaction. Stories or episodes in the lives of these other terrestrial leaders were preserved on the tablet records, which tells us that sex-oriented behavior was notable enough to have been dictated to scribes who etched these stories onto clay tablets.

Nefilim lovemaking even had a set of rules that indicated with whom and for what purposes sex could take place, rules crafted on the Nefilim home planet and brought to Earth. For example, the Nefilim code allowed lovemaking between a brother and his sister, but the rules prohibited marriage between siblings with the same parentage. Interestingly, the most important sexual goal, whether leading to marriage or not, was behavior engaged in for reasons related to dynastic succession. To be eligible for succession (meaning the passing of dynastic power from one generation to the next), conception had to involve a king and his half sister, or a Nefilim offspring and his half-sister. The firstborn son of such an approved and *code-sanctioned* union usually held the right of succession to rulership—but not always.

Sexually motivated encounters were even carried out occasionally as a sovereign's privilege, such as the aggressive sexual behaviors ascribed to Gilgamesh, a demigod, when he was the young king of Uruk.* That we have tablet records of such activities, for whatever reasons they were recorded, gives us a unique way to see into Nefilim lives.

A subliminal sexual motivation dominates many of our own close interpersonal interactions, regardless of the overt purpose of the relationship. Psychologists tell us that sexual gratification is an important human *drive*† (a category of psychological motivation) and has wielded considerable influence over overt interpersonal behavior throughout human history. We learn from Sitchin's research into the ancient records that the emotion of *sexual desire* came into play long before the human species was created. Love, lovemaking, and lust come forward as passions arising out of the depths of Nefilim history. This is significant for a number of reasons, the most important of which is that this type of behavior very possibly sheds light on a genetic connection between modern humans and these ancient space travelers. Evidence suggests that this indeed is the case.

---

*This one example focused on the time when Gilgamesh was out of control in his role as king and used that position to "take" a new bride before her husband claimed his legal right to her.
†Psychologists use the term *drive* to classify human behaviors such as hunger and thirst that prompt the individual to relieve or satisfy the "state of driven tension" that the drive stimulates.

The Sexual Liaisons of the King of Nibiru

An, the king of Nibiru (known in the Akkadian language as Anu), according to implications that can be drawn from the ancient records, had a penchant for sex. We can say this with confidence because in his heavenly abode on the planet Nibiru, it is reported that his household included several sexual partners— his espoused wife and six concubines. No doubt Anu entertained each of these specially selected women in his palace, a place that was described as exhibiting great wealth, "a place with an artificial garden sculpted wholly of semiprecious stones."[2] His sexual behavior with the concubines was sanctioned by the sexual code that operated on Nibiru. His son, Enki, was born of one of these ladies, not of Anu's legal wife.

Anu's abode on Earth, also referred to as a *temple*, reportedly was situated atop a vast ziggurat that was named E.AN.NA (House of An). He used this house on the rare occasions when he came down to planet Earth accompanied by his spouse, Antu. A translator may have assigned the descriptor "temple" because Sitchin reports that it was used for religious or worshipful purposes. Likely it was a place where ceremonies were held.

One of these occasions captured Sitchin's attention. After a banquet given for the two divine visitors, Anu's consort, Antu, was taken by chaperons to the "House of the Golden Bed" and "the Divine Daughters of Anu and the Divine Daughters of Uruk" took watch outside that place all night. Anu, on the other hand, was escorted to his own quarters, a place known as Gipar. When Sitchin translated this word in both Sumerian and Akkadian, he found it designated a "taboo" place. Interestingly, in Arabic this word means "harem." When an *entu,* a chosen virgin, known also as a *hierodule*, was selected for a prearranged lovemaking tryst with a regal visitor, this was the location for that "adventure." Sexual encounters arranged on these occasions were politically motivated. The role of a hierodule, or "sacred maiden," who typically was a mortal, or perhaps a daughter of the resident king, was to have the "honor" of being bedded by the royal guest. A planned and expected sexual encounter was the vehicle for demonstrating political accord, mutual benefit, and even political trust.

However, when Anu made a visit to a place called Kullab, it was *not* a mortal female who chose to wait for him in that special chamber. It was Ishtar, Enlil's granddaughter, one of Anu's love interests (our inference here is that his sexual motivation was prompted by love). Sitchin tells us that she even went up to his heavenly abode at least twice, but no purposes were recorded for those trips. Ishtar was known for her sexual proclivities and flamboyant sexual behaviors, which no doubt did not go unnoticed by Anu.

Having taken a liking to Ishtar, Anu gave her the title, IN.AN.NA, which meant "Beloved of An." One source tells us

Fig. 4.1. Inanna/Ishtar; pictograms that accompany tablet texts frequently depict her unclothed from the waist down.

much more was involved in that intimate gesture than great-grandfatherly admiration. When Anu bequeathed his Earth-based temple to Inanna/Ishtar, Sitchin tells us that ancient gossip indicated that "she was beloved by Anu in more than platonic ways."[3] An amorous relationship of some duration developed between these two, despite the seemingly great distance between their ages.

It is reported that the idea of Inanna sleeping with the king, and repeatedly receiving the *honor* of sleeping with him, was hers. Apparently these trysts were sessions Inanna designed, perhaps for other than love-related reasons, at least on her part. The texts tell us their intimate relationship was "not at all Anu's idea—but that of Inanna herself. It was through the other gods that she was introduced to Anu, and it was they who persuaded Anu to agree."[4] Obviously Inanna was using sex for political purposes, something she did regularly. Sitchin tells us that Anu basked in the joy of having Inanna for his beloved. A tablet from Uruk (now in the Louvre Museum) describes Inanna/Ishtar as "clothed with love, feathered with seduction, a goddess of joy."[5] It is notable that this intergenerational love relationship was not regarded as negative; this type of familial sexual relationship was not even considered to be incest as it would be in our society.

Anu did not live in his Earth-based temple (except for occasional visits), so when this temple was given to Inanna/Ishtar as a reward, it did not interfere with his visits. The Sumerian texts tell us that Anu gave Inanna his temple as "a gift of betrothal."[6] There is no mention of a follow up to that line, so we do not know if Anu did more than espouse her with an extravagant gesture. It is not a stretch of credulity to assume that Inanna made good use of her somewhat attenuated relationship with the King of Nibiru, both personally and politically. But it is likely that

Anu's senses indeed were filled with this seductive female because love consumes reason.

The Sexual Behavior of Enlil, the Chief Anunnaki Leader

In *The 12th Planet* Sitchin recounts a sexual encounter involving Enlil, who became the supreme leader of the Anunnaki mission after he was brought to Earth by his father, the king of Nibiru. As the rightful heir of the king and as "Lord of the Command," he was a Nefilim leader of considerable political stature. Yet according to Sitchin's interpretation of the account given in a Sumerian tablet, in this episode he succumbed to what is described as a lustful sexual temptation.

The text describes Enlil's chance encounter with an Anunnaki woman with whom he became smitten. It was love at first sight when he saw her naked as she bathed in a stream near his dwelling. He was consumed—his head, heart, and physical senses were infected by the sight of this girl—and his moral judgment was squeezed out of his thoughts by his sexual desire. The tablet text is self-explanatory:

> *The shepherd Enlil, who decrees the fates,*
> *The Bright Eyed One, saw her.*
> *The lord speaks to her of intercourse;*
> *She is unwilling.*
> *Enlil speaks to her of intercourse;*
> *she is unwilling:*
> *"My vagina is too small [she said],*
> *It knows no copulation;*

My lips are too little,
they know not kissing."[7]

The tablet evidence indicates that Enlil's first encounter with this young Anunnaki girl took place on the banks of a stream near his city of Nippur, no doubt a fairly public location. It also tells us that when he saw this girl naked, he immediately *fell in love*, but not necessarily with marriage in mind. Clearly, his concern was for the moment, and did not take into account any consequences for his future, or that of the girl's, suggesting his emotion at the outset was *not* one of love, but that of *lust*.

According to the code of acceptable Nefilim sexual behavior there were serious consequences for anyone who engaged in sex that was not by mutual consent. But what happened to Enlil (apparently) is that his sexual desire overrode any thoughts of personal repercussions. The maiden's refusal did not dissuade him. Enlil disclosed to his chamberlain his burning desire to *have* this young maiden.[8] The chamberlain suggested to his lord that he take the girl out on his boat. Subsequently, Enlil did persuade the girl to go sailing with him, and once they were afloat, *he raped her.*

Moral law within the Anunnaki culture did not conscience such a violent act, and even the fact that Enlil was the supreme leader in charge of the Earth-based mission did not afford him any protection or leniency; he still was censured. His outraged underlings seized him, shouting "Enlil, immoral one! Get thyself out of the city!"[9] He was subsequently sentenced to punishment. They banished him to the "Lower World," which was the designation for Africa where the mining activity was located. Sitchin tells this event with this interesting choice of words: "He was as any young man enticed by a naked beauty."

The act of censure and subsequent banishment bespeaks a moral code that was revered widely in Anunnaki society, and which *applied to all*, including the most powerful Nefilim leader.

But, as fate would have it, the girl, SUD, found herself pregnant with Enlil's child, so she followed him to his place of banishment. Enlil must have felt encouraged by the effort that Sud made to find him. He likely saw it as an indication of her acceptance—and perhaps love—for him. It is entirely possible that his *lust* shifted to responsible *love and caring* because Enlil then married her.

This story has more than one version, according to Sitchin's research. In the second version of this event, it is the girl who is the seducer, at the urging of her mother. However, Sitchin tells it this way: "Regardless of how they *fell for each other*"[10] the final outcome of this encounter is the same in both versions: Enlil married the girl. Following the marriage, Sud was given appropriate rank and received the name NIN.LIL, a name befitting a goddess. She also received what the text calls "the garment of ladyship" and thereafter was held in highest esteem among the Anunnaki. Based on Enlil's subsequent faithful follow through, which extended well into their future, perhaps his initial emotion indeed was *true love*; it just was expressed in an urgent, obsessed, or lustfully driven manner at the outset. Another possibility is that his overt sexual desire indeed was love.

Apparently, this event was the first and *almost* last out-of-wedlock sexual encounter in which Enlil engaged. There were no other tales of sexual relationships (except one) involving Enlil recorded in any of the numerous tablet collections Sitchin examined, except one. The one other case of Enlil's out-of-wedlock sexual behavior apparently had to do with dynastic succession.

The ending of this story seems to indicate that *fidelity* existed within Nefilim culture, but, perhaps thinking more critically, it was a personal belief in fidelity that tells us more about Enlil's personality and personal restraint (or fear of punishment) than about sexual norms among the Nefilim and Anunnaki.

Enki's Sexual Exploits

The sexual exploits of the other highborn leader of the Nefilim, Enki, follow a much different pattern. Enki was what Sitchin called a "persistent philanderer," due to his incorrigible and indomitable sexual behaviors. His most shameful encounters clearly were motivated by his efforts to secure access to the Divine Throne so that his firstborn offspring would have the ability to gain dominion over Earth. While he understood that the laws of succession ruled out his own chance, he was dedicated to securing this valuable heritage for an heir. The ancient texts imply that Enki became obsessed with producing a male heir of the correct bloodline who would be a third-generation successor.[11]

Enki had a longstanding lust for his half sister, Ninhursag, who was Anu's daughter, therefore a half sister to both himself and Enlil. The tablets tell us she also was "of the heavens," meaning born on Nibiru. When he became obsessed with producing a son under the terms of the succession code, he focused on having a child by Ninhursag. She was reported to have been very beautiful in her youth. More important, she also was a "woman of property," a very valuable property—the territory known as Sinai.

When Earth's domains were divided between Anu's offspring, Ninhursag was given the Land of Dilmun (the Sinai Peninsula), the location of the very important postdiluvial spaceport. This was the place from where gold was transshipped to Nibiru. After the drawing of lots to assign the rest of the globe to Enki and Enlil, the Sinai was put under the protective custody of Ninhursag by her father, Anu. In order to shield the site from frivolous outbreaks of jealousy and aggression between Enki and Enlil, whose domains both bordered the spaceport lands, Anu gave them to his respected and peace-loving female offspring, Ninhursag, essentially for safekeeping.

In a text studied by Sitchin, named "Enki and Ninhursag—a Paradise Myth," Enki once traveled to Dilmun for conjugal purposes with Ninhursag. His half sister was unmarried, and alone there.[12] In preparation for his "sexual advances" toward her, and fueled by his intention to produce a son from this half sister, he instructed the underlings to be aware that he and Ninhursag were not to be disturbed. Then, he summarily inseminated her. It is entirely possible that she had great affection for Enki. There is no evidence to support the contention that she held the emotion of "love" for him, but that possibility does exist.

After "the nine months of Womanhood" (the text's description of pregnancy), Ninhursag produced a *daughter*. Enki must have been thoroughly chagrined. In the following small excerpt from the Sitchin text that relates Enki's recorded actions, the ellipses indicate gaps in the original text:

A long tale relates how Enki, seeking a male son by his half-sister . . . forced his attentions on her when she was alone and "poured the semen in the womb." When she gave birth to a daughter, Enki lost no time making love to the girl as soon as she became "young and fair". . . . He took his joy of her, he embraced her, lay in her lap, he touches the thighs, he touches the . . . with the young one he cohabits."[13]

Enki's behavior and the text record suggest he was *in love* with this girl. But, his determined effort to produce a son obviously had become a sexual obsession. The language in the tablets indicates he demonstrated either *infatuation* or *love* (or both) toward Ninhursag's daughter during his efforts to impregnate her. Enki's behavior was likely unconsciously fueled by the emotional wounds he carried, no doubt originating when he discovered that he had been shut out of succession (a situation over which he had no control). This situation with Ninhursag's daughter was repeated again with Ninhursag's granddaughter, strongly suggesting that his feelings about his ineligible background left him with a deep psychological trauma that he wanted to alleviate, somehow, by producing a son within a correct bloodline. To accomplish this, Enki used the only capability over which he had control—sex.

Sitchin points out that the tablets tell us that the same code of conduct that condemned rape did *not* prohibit extramarital affairs. No doubt Enki believed his behavior adhered correctly to the Anunnaki moral code. That code permitted the Nefilim to have any number of wives and concubines.[14] However, when Enki went after (no doubt lustfully) the daughter of Ninhursag, and then that daughter's female child, whose conception he also was responsible for, his espoused one, his wife Ninki/Damkina, put a curse on him.* She gave him some plants to eat that made him

---

*In Sitchin's several works, the actions of cursing Enki and feeding him a poisonous plant are ascribed to two different females. Whoever it was who actually made him mortally ill and stopped his obsession is not important; what was important was the result.

mortally ill, and paralyzed him. No further information is given to explain how this was carried out, or the identity of the plant, but it did stop his seemingly compulsive sexual behavior.

Enki's generationally repetitious sexual actions do support our assumption that his behavior indicated a psychologically motivated obsession. Remember, his expected rights for control of Earth had been usurped by Enlil's presence. Anu seemingly held no consideration for the work Enki did developing the gold procurement mission and seemed to show no appreciation for his role in settling and developing the habitats of Earth. It took a powerful physiological shock, an event Enki likely perceived as a "near death experience," to break Enki's sexual preoccupation and put to rest his compulsive behavior.*

Enki was not without male offspring, but none were offspring of the union with his half sister. His firstborn son, Marduk, was conceived with his official consort. He produced five additional sons, but none of these births allowed these progeny to challenge Enlil's son, Ninurta, for succession. Ninurta was born of Enlil and Ninhursag (Ninmah), his half sister.† Both Enlil and Ninmah were *unmarried* at the time of Ninurta's conception, but Ninurta was of the correct bloodline to be eligible for succession as Enlil's rightful heir.

---

*This story implies the extreme longevity of Nefilim life-spans. Aging did not effectively diminish Enki's sex drive, as would be the case for earthlings. We also remember the Bible's list of extremely long life-spans of several generations, which seemed characteristic of some metabolic process that no longer exists for the majority of the human population. No matter how old Enki was during these events, he showed extraordinary determination to achieve his goal, but all for naught.

†According to Sitchin's research, Ninmah had several names, among them Ninhursag and Mammu, a name that Sitchin tells us is the forerunner of *mom* or *mama*. Uncharacteristically—for those from Nibiru—she never married.

Inanna—The Goddess of Love

Inanna/Ishtar makes her first appearance in Sitchin's books as the goddess who aided the Hittites in some of their battles. She was known as the "Lady of the Battlefield," and Sitchin tells us that the records indicate that it was due to her "divine power" that many a victory was attributed to her when she "came down" from the skies to "smite" the hostile countries. Likely this was a reference to her ability to "fly above" the Earth in an airborne vehicle.* Nevertheless, it was Inanna's reputation as an enticing seductress that gave her fighting powers their notoriety.

In her own voice, Inanna describes her passionate relationship with her own brother:

> *My beloved met me,*
> *took his pleasure of me, rejoiced together with me.*
> *The brother brought me to his house,*
> *made me lie on its sweet bed . . .*
> *In unison, the tongue-making in unison,*
> *my brother of fairest face made fifty times.*[15]

Sitchin explains that this brother/sister lovemaking relationship can be understood to be within conventional limits because it followed acceptable practice according to the Anunnaki code. While lovemaking between full brother and sister was allowable under the moral code, *marriage* between such siblings was not. When mar-

---

*Vehicles that flew in the skies were commonly referred to in the ancient clay tablet records. These artifacts attested to the fact that the Anunnaki had what we would consider "ancient flying technology."

riage was her goal, Ishtar selected Dumuzi to be her bridegroom. The texts indicate that he was a son of Enki, and she a granddaughter of Enlil. Sitchin likens this pairing to the tale of Romeo and Juliet, and—similarly to Shakespeare's tale—the Inanna/Dumuzi relationship "ended in tragedy, death and revenge."[16] However, her choice of Dumuzi as her spouse *was* approved by her father, Nannar/Sin, and her brother Utu/Shamash. The ancient records tell us *she was deeply in love* with Dumuzi.

A tender episode is recounted between Inanna and Dumuzi when she traveled to Egypt. It appears in a text dealing with the First Pyramid War, a conflict whose roots were in "the never-ending struggle for control over Earth and its space facilities."[17] She is said to have made a battlefield appearance, but her actual intention for the visit to Egypt, Sitchin surmises, was to visit Dumuzi, who was known by the epithet "The Herder." The text indicates he awaited Inanna's arrival with anticipation:

> *The young lad stood waiting;*
> *Dumuzi pushed open the door.*
> *Like a moonbeam she came forth to him . . . .*
> *He looked at her, rejoiced in her,*
> *Took her in his arms and kissed her.*
> *The Herder put his arm around the maiden.*[18]

After the second Pyramid War—which pitted the two principal sons of Enlil and Enki (Ninurta and Marduk, respectively) and their forces against each other—Inanna's relationship was jeopardized by the fact that Dumuzi was of Enki's lineage and she was a granddaughter of Enlil. The rivalry between two clans showed itself and Inanna had to be separated from her lover. But when that warring conflict was terminated, she reunited with Dumuzi. The text tells us that they spent numerous days and nights "in bliss and ecstasy." She whispers to Dumuzi:

> *As sweet as your mouth are your parts,*
> *They befit a princely status!*
> *Subdue the rebellious country, let the nation*
> *   multiply;*
> *I will direct the country rightly!*[19]

When the background family hostilities and conflicts were heightened, the relationship between Inanna and Dumuzi turned into an unhappy one. Sitchin implies that Marduk (Enki's first-born son) was opposed to the union from the start. Most important, the relationship did not produce an heir, which was essential for carrying out the ambitions of both partners. Dumuzi even resorted to a tactic used by his father, Enki—to have intercourse with his own sister in order to conceive a son. The sister refused him, and he violated the taboo in the code and raped her. Apparently Inanna was privy to his premeditated act. He had a dream that foretold that he would be captured by bandits, and it came true. After this rape episode, Marduk seized and punished Dumuzi.[20] When Dumuzi tried to escape capture, he was killed.

Inanna/Ishtar continued to be known for her seductiveness and her sexual exploits. She was also known for her political cunning. Once, with political motives in her scheming mind, she visited E.A. (Enki), who was living on the shores of the Persian Gulf, alone and in semi-isolation. Sitchin tells that E.A. was "keeping track of human affairs, dispensing knowledge and civilization to mankind."[21] The text indicates how Inanna prepared

Fig. 4.2. Inanna flying to the lower world to meet Enki.

for this visit; she was "enchanting and perfumed." Ea/Enki was "enamored and drunk."[22]

Inanna wanted to be a queen with subjects over whom she could carry out her ambition to rule a substantial population, so she convinced Enki to make Uruk the new center of Sumerian civilization—instead of Kish, the city where kingship then was located. She reasoned that if Uruk could be her cult center, it would need to be a full-fledged urban center. But to achieve that she needed some "equipment" referred to as the MEs. What she really wanted was to reign where it really mattered, in Sumer, not where her home was then, in the far-off Indus valley. So she hatched a plan (probably long before she arrived at Enki's abode) to make Uruk her place that "really mattered."

The Sitchin text tells us that the MEs were "objects that held all the knowledge and other aspects of a high civilization." Sitchin admitted, in print and often in his presentations, especially when he discussed Inanna, that *he did not know* exactly what the MEs were, and he admitted he searched far and deep into Sumerian sources without any success; the key to what this knowledge actually was still is not specifically known. Sitchin surmised they were "some kind of computer disks or memory chips which, in spite of their minute size, hold vast amounts of information."[23] Sitchin has this to say about his conjectures relative to the coveted MEs:

> Though they are constantly referred to, the nature of the ME is not clear, and scholars translate the term as "divine commandments," "divine powers," or even "mythic virtues." The ME, however, are described as physical objects that one could pick up and carry, or even put on [like a backpack], and which contained secret knowledge or data. Perhaps they were something like our present-day computer chips, on which data, programs, and operational orders have been minutely recorded. On them the essentials of civilization were encoded.[24]

Inanna traveled in her "Boat of Heaven" (probably a small spaceship) to southeastern Africa to meet with Enki, who had secreted the ME away to that place.[25] Enki realizes she will be unchaperoned, "the maiden, all alone, has directed her step to the Abzu."[26] He orders his chamberlain to have "plenty of sweet date wine" on hand and to prepare a banquet. The Sitchin text continues:

> After Inanna and Enki had feasted and Enki's heart became happy with drink, Inanna brought up the subject of the MEs. Gracious with drink, Enki presented to her [some MEs that would make Uruk a seat of Kingship] ME for "Lordship . . . Godship, the Exalted and Enduring Tiara, the throne of Kingship," and "bright Inanna took them." As Inanna worked her charms on her aging host, Enki made to her a second presen-

tation of "the Exalted Scepter and Staff, the Exalted Shrine, and Righteous Rulership": and "bright Inanna took them," too.[27]

As the feasting and drinking went on, Enki parted with another seven MEs that provided for the functions and attributes of a Divine Lady, which would give her the status of a Great Goddess: a temple and its rituals, priests, and attendants; justice and courts; music and arts; masonry and woodworking; metalworking, leatherwork, and weaving; scribeship and mathematics; and last but not least, weapons and the art of warfare.[28]

As we recount this discussion in the words from Sitchin's text, it becomes obvious that the coveted information was of two types: detailed plans and *explicit procedures* for how to entertain royalty with the accouterments befitting a knowledgeable and legitimate royal hostess, and *blueprints* on how to *make* the ornaments of decoration that indicated kingship, namely the *tiara, scepter, and staff* as well as the shrine on which to display them. Also, this ME information must have included descriptions of how to: carry out rituals; administer justice; play music; create arts; and how to craft and display objects of masonry, woodworking, metal, leather, and weaving. And this computer information included how to make and display weapons of warfare.

What is really interesting is that recently (2012–2013), the technology for a new type of device, one that can "construct" material objects, has been invented and is gaining notoriety. Known as a 3-D printer, it is capable of making objects.* It is entirely possible

---

*One of the first objects that the 3-D printer was reported to have constructed was a working gun made of plastic. In a news report from NASA in 2014 a 3-D printer aboard the International Space Station is used to make replacement parts for the station. (See http://goo.gl/K9TyQd.)

that the coveted information contained in the MEs was blueprints for how to build such a computer and how to program it to accomplish the actual production of significant objects from various types of material. There is no way to know if the ME was chip technology (as Sitchin surmises) or if it is something more, but—if we are correct in our interpretation, that this newly developed modern computer was in fact in use in ancient times—this would mean that indeed "modern science has finally caught up with ancient knowledge."

Sitchin also explains what Enki did when he sobered up and realized what his generosity—albeit his intoxicated generosity—had done. He ordered his chamberlain to retrieve the MEs. Inanna already had given these valuable "items of her conquest" to her two pilots who flew them to Uruk. She, clever lady that she was, went to a different city, Eridu. While she kept the pursuers arguing with her in Eridu, the people of Uruk, who had received the MEs, were so grateful for the elements of "kingship and civilization" she procured for their city that they wrote a hymn of thanks to Inanna's cleverness. It was titled *Lady of the MEs*. They recited a congratulatory hymn responsively in the congregation on festival days thereafter.

The Sitchin sources did not indicate whether Enki actually seduced Inanna—or not—but Sitchin conjectures that, based on her sexual experiences with Anu and others, a dalliance did occur. If that was not the case, Sitchin was quite sure that her "femininity was aroused." Enki's inebriated state no doubt is why we have no tablet information about his follow up on this con that Inanna pulled off, but he no doubt lamented his gullibility to be so taken advantage of for a long time thereafter.

Inanna had still another sexual plan in mind, which she carried out when she made her move to Uruk, essentially abandoning her city, Aratta, located in the Indus Valley. The new king of Uruk was Enmerkar (known as "He Who Built Uruk"). He vied with the king of Aratta over Inanna. The sources tell us "the prize was not simply where Inanna would spend her time—but also where she would engage in lovemaking with the king."[29] Inanna had her regal bed identified in both cities. She indeed was a clever temptress, one who did what was important to ensure her future personal sexual "satisfactions."

Perhaps the most interesting example of Inanna's sexual capers is the one in which she was *unsuccessful* in carrying out a seduction. The setting was an encounter with Gilgamesh in the Cedar Mountains (located in what now is Lebanon). Gilgamesh was journeying to the "Landing Place." There he was seeking to get on a spaceship to go to Nibiru, where he hoped to gain immortality. He was well informed that on Nibiru, life was "eternal" and he was obsessed with the idea of avoiding mortal death. Sitchin made a study of Gilgamesh, whom he later celebrated in his novel, *The King Who Refused to Die*, based on tablet sources.

Inanna watched him from her "sky chamber" as he disrobed to wash himself after his victory in a heavy battle with the fierce mechanical guardian who protected the spaceport. Inanna approached him and made an offer for a sexual relationship using these words: "Come let us enjoy your vigor! Put your hand and touch my vulva!"[30] Gilgamesh, having heard about her exploits, and being obsessed with his own personal goal, taunted her: "Will you love me and then treat me just like [the others]?" He knew of her "throw away" treatment with a series of lovers. In other words, *he flatly refused her offer.*[31]

*Fig.4.3. Cylinder seal pictogram: Inanna observing
Gilgamesh from her skychamber.*

This likely was a first for Inanna, no doubt one that sent her
into a sexual frenzy to prove to herself she was still a sexually
attractive prize, a status she more than likely had come to highly
value. No text has been found to support this conjecture, and
Sitchin does not draw this conclusion, but it does seem logical,
given her record of prior successful sexual conquests. An often-
repeated adage is likely a fitting end to this story as it gives us a
plausible conclusion: "Hell hath no fury like a woman scorned."
Sadly, we have no texts to support it.

Inanna still engaged in one more notable relationship that
brought positive changes to the land of Mesopotamia as recorded on
the historical artifacts. The tablet text given here is the "voice" of a
gardener, later known as Sharru-kin, a precursor to his better-known
name—Sargon of Akkad. The tablets tell us of their meeting.

> *One day my queen,*
> *After crossing heaven, crossing Earth—*
> *Inanna—*

After crossing heaven, crossing Earth—
The hierodule approached weary, fell asleep.
I saw her from the edge of my garden.
I kissed her, copulated with her.[32]

Sitchin tells us that since she was asleep when this sexual encounter occurred, it cannot have been "love at first sight." However, he concludes that she must have really liked this man and his lovemaking because she invited him into her bed, and gave him the throne of Sumer. This relationship—no doubt a love relationship—lasted fifty-four (Earth) years. Sargon goes on to say: "I was a gardener, Ishtar granted me her love, and four and fifty years. I exercised kingship; the Black-Headed people I ruled and governed." Sitchin comments further that the records do not explain how Inanna persuaded the Nefilim to "entrust Sumer and its people to "the man whose kiss changed history."[33] Sargon was a very successful king. He enlarged the territory of his rule, and this, in essence, allowed him to establish the first historically known empire. It extended from the Mediterranean to the Persian Gulf and became what later was called Assyria.[34]

The Sexual Attraction of the Daughters of Men

A short time before the event known as "Noah's Flood," the population on Earth had increased to give rise to huge noisy throngs carousing in the city streets. To exacerbate the situation, Earth's food supply had become so taxed by the burgeoning human population—causing widespread hunger and desperation—that some people even resorted to cannibalism. Enlil was so dismayed by these consequences of sexually driven procreation, he entreated Enki to take measures to alleviate the suffering. Enlil subsequently took matters into his own hands. He planned to take drastic action to erase earthlings from the planet. He decided to let the Deluge wipe humankind off the Earth.

At nearly the same time, or perhaps just before, unrest erupted on the space platforms where Anunnaki astronauts monitored Earth. The three hundred Anunnaki (known as Igigi) who manned the space stations that orbited Earth complained they had no opportunity for respite from their duties. Their long tours of duty that kept them aloft precluded access to females, a situation that contributed to their grievances. When some of these Igigi (Those Who Observe and See) were allowed to come down to Earth, it did not take long before they observed that the females born of humans were fair and enticing. This tablet excerpt explains the situation that developed:

> *And it came to pass,*
> *When the Earthlings began to increase in number*
> *upon the face of the Earth,*
> *and daughters were born unto them,*
> *That the sons of the Elohim*
> *saw the daughters of the Earthlings*
> *that they were compatible.*
> *And they took unto themselves*
> *wives of whatever they chose.*[35]

This was a new era for the Nefilim leaders, and Enlil was incensed by intermarriage between the Anunnaki and earthlings. We already have discussed his wish to let them be destroyed by the natural flooding and Enki's actions to save a few in the ark (in chapter 2). Suffice it to say that Enlil's initial anger at finding some earthlings as survivors of the Deluge was short lived. The surviving Nefilim and Anunnaki pointed out how useful earthlings had become, and how important they were to doing the work that provided the Nefilim food supply. So, he accepted them and bade them to "go forth and multiply." This story is well known in biblical history so we will not repeat it here.

Genetic Evidence of the Human-Anunnaki Connection?

What do we learn from these sexual escapades chronicled in such detail by Sitchin, all drawn from the Sumerian tablets? One important thing this body of information tells us is that the emotion of *love* is an ancient one. Another less obvious implication suggests that Nefilim (and perhaps Anunnaki) men—like earthling men— think of sex regularly and recurrently, and even obsessively. One important difference between human preoccupations with sex is that it often is aimed at pleasure (not just reproduction). Ordinary earthlings are not dealing with succession issues; their emotions are relatively uncomplicated by such political and dynastic concerns.

Clearly, *gratification* is the seemingly essential goal of sexual relationships, one no doubt sought by both Nefilim and humans. Relatively recently, scientists have found that the presence of a specific gene is statistically associated with *sexual desire.** This is important information that serves to give validity to the

---

*In 2006, a report on research done at the University of Jerusalem by Richard Ebstein was published. The research found a small but *statistically significant* influence of the gene DRD4, associated with *sexual desire*, on human behavior. This proves that sexual desires are not completely psychological, as previously thought.

conjecture that humans inherited sexual desire, the forerunner of most actual sexual actions. The last two chapters of Sitchin's 2010 book, *There Were Giants Upon the Earth,* are devoted to his hopes for future scientific proof of a genetic relationship between the Nefilim and modern humans, which would explain the root of not only *sexual desire,* but a host of human emotional predilections.* Perhaps genetic information also will reveal a causal linkage between humans and the Nefilim for emotions such as aggressiveness, hate, jealousy, envy, and selfishness.

One emotion has already been found to have a proven genetic origin: "shyness," which was previously judged to be a behavioral tendency under conscious behavioral control. Finding a gene responsible for shyness holds promise that genetic roots of a plethora of human emotional behaviors might be discovered. As genetic scientists uncover more about the structure and function of the human genome, we will be able to learn more about possible sources of human behavior. Without doubt, we will need to return to the questions posed here with this new information in hand to see if and in what ways our conjectures are correct—that we have "inherited" sexual proclivities, as well as other traits and behaviors—from the Nefilim.

The work of Zecharia Sitchin has set out such a possible and plausible future for our consideration, and we can be thankful for having his contribution to prepare us for other possible, probable, plausible, and preferable future scenarios.

---

*In *There Were Giants Upon the Earth,* Sitchin discussed his efforts to have the mummy of Nin.Puabi, an Anunnaki queen, whose remains were found shelved in unopened boxes at the British Museum in London, examined for mitochondrial DNA links from Anu to Enlil to Ninmah/Ninhursag to Bau/Gula. This project still is awaiting action as of the publication (2016) of this book.

5

Wonderful Flying Machines

Of course the flying saucers are real, and they are interplanetary.

AIR CHIEF MARSHAL LORD DOWDING,
HEAD OF ROYAL AIR FORCE DURING WWII,
QUOTED BY REUTERS, AUGUST 1954

Statistically it's a certainty there are hugely advanced civilizations, intelligences, and life forms out there. I believe it's possible they even came here.

ASTRONAUT STORY MUSGRAVE

The American public and their leaders (and perhaps others around the world) struggle with the question of whether saucer-like flying vehicles seen occasionally in Earth's skies are real, tangible objects, and if so, whether they traversed interplanetary space to show up in Earth's atmosphere. Expert voices like that of astronaut Story Musgrave and Air Chief Marshal Lord Dowding attest that sighted space vehicles indeed *are real*. Furthermore, these vehicles traveled deep space to get to the remote portion of the galaxy where our Earth is orbiting. Thousands of expert and lay observers already have attested to the veracity of such observations.

Military and airline personnel, scientists, astronauts, space experts, and ordinary citizens have made credible sightings of flying objects that can slip into another dimension in the blink of an eye. Other seemingly fantastic sightings have been well documented by thousands. Notable is an event that was observed over Phoenix, Arizona known as the Phoenix Lights. The vehicle that was seen was huge. Even the then governor of that state saw it block out almost all of the sky.* Experts and laypeople have *identified* many intergalactic flying vehicles, and their collective judgments are that indeed they are real, tangible objects and are made of "unearthly" substances such as metals not able to be made on Earth with our current technology.

Another person who can speak from personal experience is Travis Walton, a fellow taken aboard one of these vehicles on November 5, 1975, while he was working as a logger in the mountains of Arizona. When I spoke to him after his presentation at the International UFO Conference, he said, "Yes, of course UFOs are real. I *saw* a vehicle, and I even was abducted and kept on a UFO for five days."

Despite the thousands of comments from credible witnesses, hundreds of thousands continue to doubtfully ask this question: "If these objects are actual vehicles that travel across space, did

---

*Governor Fife Symington, in a 2007 article by Leslie Kean, made this statement about the event that occurred on March 13, 1997: "I'm a pilot and I know just about every machine that flies. It was bigger than anything that I've *ever seen*. It remains a great mystery. Other people saw it, responsible people. I don't know why people would ridicule it."

they *really* come from another planet? If so, how?" In the context of advances in space science research, such questions reveal understandings that are way out of touch with recent scientific findings. Most of us have learned that outer space contains objects (like planets, star systems, and galaxies) located light years away. This measure presumes space is traversed in a linear manner, as one would travel a mile or kilometer on Earth. The light-year measurement implies large amounts of time needed to traverse outer space. However, we are in the kindergarten of our learning about intergalactic travel.

The fields of celestial mechanics and astrophysics have *disproved* the notion that interplanetary travel is all but impossible. What is outmoded is the belief that linear distances preclude travel to other star systems. Scientists from space-oriented disciplines tell us that *space is curved** and that "wormholes" allow travel from seemingly distant realms of outer space that are actually *not* so far away that vehicles cannot reach the vicinity of Earth. This means that the notion of the linear measurement of distance (i.e., light years) implying huge amounts of travel time is *no longer the way astrophysicists think of distances in outer space.* It is this new way of conceptualizing space travel that explains how observed vehicles got here.

We are forced to ask an obvious question: What type—or amount—of evidence will it take to persuade the huge body of skeptics (and the American government and military) to accept the concept of interplanetary travel as a reality? Perhaps we can

---

*Using Einstein's general theory of relativity, scientific research is showing how gravity is a force that draws mass into a curved trajectory. See discussion at: "Theories of the Universe: Curved Space," www.infoplease.com/cig/theories-universe/curved-space.html.

find convincing evidence in the books written by one who has studied very ancient history and the ancient Sumerian knowledge. Such a knowledgeable researcher was Zecharia Sitchin.

Documentable ancient evidence identified by Sitchin's extensive study of ancient clay tablet records tells us that Earth *already* has experienced centuries of flying vehicles plying the space we know as Earth's skies, and also that our planet historically has accommodated vehicles capable of flying from—and to—other planets. The message given by the ancient clay tablet sources studied by Sitchin is clear: many thousands of years ago, flying machines of several types were used by a group of technologically *advanced* astronauts who came to Earth from another inhabited planet. Sitchin's books are peppered with descriptive explanations that depict the use of flying vehicles by these ancient settlers. In this chapter we will select examples that bring forward reports of several types of flying vehicles used in a variety of ways.

Gold Transport Missions

As we have seen, the leaders, the Nefilim, and workers who called themselves the Anunnaki, came to this planet to obtain gold that was needed on their home planet. Earth's gold was first mined, then shipped from South Africa to Sumer. From there it went to the Sinai where it was smelted and prepared for transshipment to Nibiru. Sitchin gives us this report of what the ancient records tell us.

> The complex system of space operations [tracked] the comings and goings by the space vehicles and communications between Earth and Nibiru, while both planets pursued their own destined orbits [that were] coordinated from Enlil's Mission

Control Center in Nippur. There, atop a raised platform, was the DIR.GA room, the most restricted "holy of holies," where the vital celestial charts and orbital data panels—the "Tablets of Destinies" were installed.[1]

The king of Nibiru, Anu, had sent his firstborn son, Enki, to Earth for gold. This decision implies that the Nibiruans already were aware of the fact that Earth held a considerable supply of that metal. The key question is: How did they know this? Sitchin gives us an array of possibilities.

> They could have probed Earth with unmanned satellites, as we have been doing to other planets in our solar system. They could have surveyed Earth by landing on it, as we have done on our Moon. Indeed, their landing on Mars cannot be ruled out as we read texts dealing with the space voyages from Nibiru to Earth.[2]

What is important about Sitchin's reports is that the Nibiruans had to have had very advanced technology in order to carry out probes of a planetary surface. To use Mars as a base or way station meant those from Nibiru had solved the problem of how to survive and perhaps live with very low levels of oxygen and gravity that we know exist on that planet (if indeed it had the levels of atmosphere our scientists have found with their probes). To travel anywhere in space implies—no! documents—that the Anunnaki came from a *very* advanced space-oriented and highly developed technological civilization.

Now comes the clincher: *these space travels across interplanetary space and into Earth space began some 445,000 years ago. Modern science is just beginning to develop travel and exploration capabilities like those that were in use thousands of years ago.* In Sitchin's first book, *The 12th Planet,* he begins his fifth chapter with these words: "Sumerian and Akkadian texts *leave no doubt* that the peoples of the ancient Near East were certain that the Gods of Heaven and Earth were able to rise from Earth and ascend into the heavens, as well as roam Earth's skies at will (emphasis added)."[3]

Just as modern space flight activities have mission control centers that monitor flight operations from which commands are issued and information is received, the ancient space missions had their DIR.GA control center containing astronomical information, (likely) in digital form, used to monitor and guide space operations. Because of the multiple types of vehicles and different segments of deep space Anunnaki vehicles traversed, it is safe to assume that their control functions used complex databases and multiple "command and control" procedures that we have begun to use in Earth's space programs. Likely our modern space flight procedures still are much simpler than those used in ancient times. In modern times, for launches, typically only one vehicle at a time is launched and requires monitoring. The Anunnaki had spaceports that likely functioned like our modern hub airports with traffic coming and going simultaneously (or at least in close succession).

The Flying Goddess

There perhaps is one indisputable example of Nefilim capabilities with flight, and it is the one associated with the goddess Inanna/Ishtar. She was renowned for her courage on the battlefield and for her use of vehicles that allowed her attacks to emanate from "above," from the skies. Her travel activities also were highlighted in many of the ancient tablets describing her use of flight. Sitchin tells us she is described as "roaming the heavens over many lands that lie far apart—feats possible only by *flying*."[4] She was shown in an ancient cylinder seal depiction to have wings on her image, and with her on one of these pictograms is her grandfather, E.A./Enki (shown with his characteristic water streams containing fish that were used as his identification). This characteristic image conveys the message that Ishtar typically moved from place to place by flight.[5]

She also is described as regularly using her "Boat of Heaven," but frequently she used her MU, which may have been a more technical term for the technology she had on board. The MU (meaning "that which rises straight," and, as clarified by Sitchin, "sky vehicle") could hover in Earth's skies, or become a "command module," or even fly when attached to a *gir*, which was a long arrow-shaped object divided into several compartments. These descriptions bring to the modern mind the image of an advanced helicopter, perhaps with rocket weapons mounted on its undersides.

The following hymn to Isthar/Inanna, found in the tablets, celebrates her flying vehicle:

> *Lady of Heaven:*
> *She puts on the Garment of Heaven;*
> *She valiantly ascends towards Heaven.*
> *Over all the peopled lands*
> *she flies in her MU*
> *Lady, who in her MU*
> *to the heights of Heaven joyfully wings,*
> *Over all the resting places*
> *she flies in her MU.*[6]

For some of her sky-borne adventures, Ishtar strapped to her body seven objects that obviously were technologies she needed for individual flight. This "flying gear" also included a helmet with earphones, and all these items were fastened on her before she "mounted the skies."[7] This description brings to mind modern attempts to use individual flying technology.

Ishtar's "flying" exploits are discussed frequently in Sitchin's work, probably because she was a Nefilim (goddess) who exhibited many flamboyant characteristics. After Ishtar developed her royal abode in Uruk, she still flew (using Sitchin's words) "from place to place in her 'Boat of Heaven.' Her flying about gave rise to many depictions of her as an aeronaut."[8] Her flying journeys carried the inference from some texts that she did her own piloting. However, like other major deities, she was assigned a pilot-navigator for the more demanding flights. A tablet presents an explanation in support of this fact:

> At the time when Enmerkar [the king] in Uruk
>   ruled,
> Nungal, the lion-hearted, was the Pilot
> who from the skies brought Ishtar down
> To the E-Anna.[9]

Some humans regularly saw rocketlike objects in flight. Evidence of this was found on Hittite glyphs. Pictorial evidence was found on Crete, dating to the thirteenth century BCE, which shows a flying rocket ship with flames emitting from its rear.[10] These examples of ancient artifacts give us pictorial evidence that is indisputable.

Ninurta's Divine Black Bird

In another example, Ninurta, the son of Enlil, also had a flying machine called the "Divine Black Bird." He is reported to have roamed the skies in this fast vehicle. The indication of the color black brings forth the image of modern military fighter aircraft such as the Navy F-35 Lightning II, or even the U-2 S Dragon Lady. As mentioned earlier, after the Deluge, Ninurta undertook several efforts in the mountains of Mesopotamia where water damage was rampant. Sitchin tells us that Ninurta rushed from place to place in the mountains to supervise and carry out this work, using his airship for these hurried travels, but "his *Winged Bird* on the summit was smashed, its pinions crashed down to earth."[11] He was rescued from the crash, but this incident reminds us of reports of modern military (and civilian) aircraft accidents.

Sometime around 2200 BCE in Egypt, a later king, Gudea, built a ziggurat for Ninurta. He struggled to follow the original traditional design. Troubled by not being able to initiate the project in the way it was supposed to be built, Ninurta consulted an oracle goddess, Nanshe. She told him that this new house "had to provide appropriate places for Ninurta's weapons, for his *great aircraft*, even for his favorite lyre."[12] Later, Ninurta wrote, "The dream was fulfilled . . . like a bright mass it stands, a radiant brightness of its facing covers everything; like a mountain which glows it joyously rises."[13] What is significant to note is that special enclosures or facilities for housing the Divine Black Bird were built into this structure. Also mentioned was that there was storage for Ninurta's "awesome weapons" on these grounds. To receive mention in the tablets, the supply of these weapons must have been very large. Also, apparently the wingspan on the aircraft was extremely wide—therein causing the challenge to accommodate it in the new house. The original design of a ziggurat had to be seriously modified. But Gudea finally solved this problem and Ninurta was pleased.

As mentioned earlier, when the Anunnaki and Nefilim were forced to retreat from Earth to the skies to avoid the Great Flood, they used vehicles that were rocket propelled to escape the roiling waters. The vehicles they used were described as "chariots of the gods."[14]

Teshub, "Windy Storm"

Another text describing a notable battle documents that they made use of aircraft in the fighting. A battle fought in the sky was identified in a particularly long Hittite text that dealt with a Hittite supreme deity, Teshub (a name that meant "Windy Storm"), in a battle against the evil god Kumarbi. Here is the text as recounted by Sitchin who tells us of the vehicles used in this war:

> The final battles raged in the skies and in the seas; in one battle Teshub was supported by seventy gods riding in their *chariots*. At first defeated and either hiding or exiled, Teshub finally faced his challenger in god-to-god combat. Armed with the "Thunder-stormer which scatters the rocks for ninety furlongs" and "the Lightning which flashes frightfully," he ascended skyward in his *chariot*, pulled by two gold-plated Bulls of Heaven, and "from the skies he set his face" toward his enemy. . . . Teshub was finally victorious. (emphasis added).[15]

In yet another battle fought by Teshub described in the tablet records, chariots were involved. These chariots were vehicles prepared for combat and were described in the sources being revved up with the "Great Cracker," that was attached to the "Bull," which was the power plant that "Lights Up" in front and the "Bull for Lofty Missile" was on the back end. Then a radarlike device called "That Which Shows the Way" was installed along with some powerful energy "Stones" (minerals), and the vehicle was armed with the "Storm Thunderer," and loaded with no less than eight hundred "Fire Stones."[16] Obviously this is describing fearsome airborne vehicles, particularly planes loaded with bombs. Instead of recounting the battle here (as Sitchin does), our interest will stay focused on the fact that the vehicles that fought the battle were called "aerial chariots."

This example attests to the fact that the skies were used not just for peacetime travel, but—just like in modern wars of the twentieth and twenty-first centuries—also were the battlegrounds. What is important to remember is that these airborne events took place in ancient times and were recorded on clay tablets dated to be in the vicinity of six thousand years old. While we cannot be sure specifically what all of the armaments were intended to accomplish, we can be sure from this evidence that these "chariots" were equipped with fearsome firepower.

Persistent Space Flight

This collection of events described in tablet sources allows us to acknowledge that flight—for personal travel, for interplanetary exploration, for economic and environmental purposes, and for both war and survival—existed in very ancient times on planet Earth. All these types of uses for flying vehicles put objects into the skies on a regular and recurring basis.

Tablet evidence also exists confirming that the people of the eastern Mediterranean *saw, on several occasions,* rocketlike objects in flight. While some scholars have documented (often using famous historical works of art)[17] that throughout history "flying objects" were seen in Earth's skies, the scientific age has raised a curtain of skepticism based, in part, in the methodology that requires that observations need replicable proof. Confirmation by numerous observers often is not sufficient to be considered convincing evidence. If skepticism could be put to rest, more fruitful questions could be posed that would allow us as a species to make the quantum leap that is needed to support the claim that we, Earth's inhabitants, are on the doorstep of a new era, one encompassing interplanetary travel. This likely will happen when Nibiru returns to the vicinity of Earth.

These vignettes do not exhaust all the references to space flight, space travel, and interplanetary travel that Sitchin cites in his fourteen books, but it does provide a sample—a convincing sample—to illustrate the point that *vehicles that travel across interplanetary space are not new to Earth's skies.* What modern society is calling *unidentified* flying objects are the types of vehicles that were attested to in ancient observations and written about on clay artifacts. Perhaps we earthlings were observed in ancient times, and continue to be observed from the skies in modern times also.

What is especially notable is that flying objects have been sighted in modern times near or over nuclear facilities that have malfunctioned. Documentation can be found of a UFO being seen over the Chernobyl Nuclear Power Station (ChNPS) on the night of April 26, 1986. A scientist, Dr. Vladimer Rubstov, gave the following report at a European conference and it was published in the MUFON (Mutual UFO Network) 1994 Symposium's Proceedings:

> About one month before the Chernobyl disaster I had a talk with an air traffic controller of the Kharkov airport. He told me that, according to pilots' reports, there was a rising number of UFO observations in the area of the Chernobyl Nuclear Power Station. Later it became known that on the night of the fire in the ChNPS, some 3 hours after the explosion, a team of nuclear specialists saw in the sky over the station a fiery ball of the color of brass. The witnesses estimated its diameter as 6–8 meters and its distance from the burning nuclear reactor No. 4 was some 300 meters. Just before the observation these specialists measured the level of radiation in the place where they were standing. It was measured at 3000 milliroentgens per hour. "Suddenly two bright rays of crimson color extended from the ball to the reactor. . . . . [and] lasted for some 3 minutes. . . . The rays abruptly faded and the ball slowly floated away in a northwesterly direction, towards Byelorussia. Then we again looked at our radiation monitor. It displayed only 800 milliroentgens per hour."[18]

This is an incredible report of direct UFO intervention in an Earth-based nuclear disaster. While radiation effects had killed some and spread to the region surrounding the reactor facility, obviously the huge radiation effects were mitigated by the action of the UFO.

Flying objects have been seen over several other nuclear plants around the world. Another example reports UFOs observed around the Krska Nuclear Power plant in Slovenia in 2009.

Sightings also are reported around the Mecklenburg Nuclear Plant in the U.S. state of North Carolina. Reports of similar sightings at other nuclear facilities can be found at numerous Internet sites.[19] In fact, since the late 1940s, sixteen reports of UFO sightings over atomic and nuclear power facilities have been reported.[20]

A UFO was sighted relatively recently over the Fukushima Daiishi Nuclear Power plant that suffered damage after an earthquake and tsunami hit northern Japan on March 12, 2011. Videos from various sources, showing a fleet of UFOs over the Fukushima nuclear power plant, or in its vicinity, are available.[21] It should be noted that the disaster there has lingered, and involves radiation contamination in groundwater that is flowing into the sea. Operators of this Japanese facility must keep pumping in water to prevent an explosion, which in turn creates huge amounts of radioactive water that seeps into the groundwater. The short-term solution of these hydrological problems requires those responsible to keep the water in storage tanks.[22]*

The conclusion that can be drawn from this video evidence is that UFOs are interested in Earth-based atomic and nuclear installations, with most reports of UFO sightings beginning around 1950, after nuclear weapons were used on two Japanese cities. Some observers indicate that these flying vehicles have monitoring technology to assess the safety of nuclear facilities. The Rubstov evidence (cited above) indicates these vehicles not only monitored but intervened to mitigate the radiation effects during the Chernobyl disaster. This observed behavior of UFOs

---

*In the video at the link listed in the Notes section, the commentary in Spanish notes that there has been a complete media *blackout* in Japan concerning these UFOs.

suggests benevolence toward those people who live in the vicinity of Earth's very dangerous nuclear facilities.

While attempting to link the Nefilim with these modern events, we cannot draw a connection to any Nefilim/Anunnaki sources to better understand why a UFO would show benevolence by intervening at the Chernobyl site, but we do know that Enki showed benevolence toward humans. What we do learn from this evidence is that those who use UFO vehicles are wary of humans' ability to prevent nuclear accidents. When humans showed their inventive capability to build atomic weapons in the mid-1940s, it may have signaled to the "gods" that humans needed close monitoring to prevent any future uses of such devastating weaponry.

6

War and Warring— An Earthly Inclination?

In a philosophical conversation on an American
nuclear submarine,
the executive officer was asked by the Captain
"Who is the enemy in war?"
The executive officer replies:
"The enemy of war is war itself."

CRIMSON TIDE, 1995 MOVIE
DIRECTED BY TONY SCOTT

Violence is a reaction against a situation
which has become intolerable.

IN THE SHOES OF THE FISHERMAN, 1968 MOVIE
DIRECTED BY MICHAEL ANDERSON

When the final history of humankind is written, will humans be able to offer acceptable reasons for the most provocative and destructive characteristic of human civilizations—the penchant to engage in war? Likely there is no single answer to this question, and humankind cannot offer any reason for this phenomena. One commentator on warfare tells us that "the facts of war are not cold. They burn with the heat of the fires of hell."[1] War could be considered a method of destruction on par with hurricanes, typhoons, tornados, and tsunamis. But unlike those types of natural destruction, war is a man-made form of devastation, and therefore *is preventable*. As an actor in the movie *Crimson Tide* points out, "the enemy of war is war itself." We must be reminded of one indisputable fact: wars on Earth kill those of our own species—humans. This chapter asks a provocative question in the title: Is war an earthly inclination? Are there any other possible answers to the question, "Why is war so prevalent on Earth?"

One possible justification is offered in the dialog of an interesting 1968 movie, *In the Shoes of the Fisherman*. In that drama, a Catholic cardinal discusses important issues to be dealt with by a future pope. He is challenged to offer his opinion on the use of violence and war. Certainly war is the epitome of violence launched against members of one's own species. The actor's dialogue is very revealing and stems from his deep introspection as a member of a profession that abhors killing. His viewpoint is that *violence undertaken at a personal scale sometimes is justified*. However when we consider that war typically is initiated by people in power, specifically by decision-makers who wage war for other than personal purposes, we see that war is more than a personal decision—it is a national one.

In today's world, the effects of warring no longer can be justified—by anyone, for any reason. No matter what the objective, war is intolerable for the people who "get in the way" on both sides. In today's world where sophisticated weapons are used to inflict the greatest damage on property and people, the effects of war are far removed from those who initiate war.

We must again ask the critical question: Why do humans look to war and warring to solve their territorial, ideological, political, religious, or personal disputes, when war is such an imperfect solution to any problem? One powerful reason is that *war works*. Wars typically allow victory to be achieved for someone or some group. The inhumanity of war seems not to concern the perpetrators.

These are important questions, and any answer is ineffectual and unsatisfactory. Perhaps we should broaden the focus. Is it only *human* civilizations that use war to solve huge problems? This question is impossible to answer, as we have no information about non-earthly civilizations—or do we?

When we search the academic literature for an answer to "Why war?" we find an evolutionary biologist, David Livingston Smith, telling us that his research points to the fact that "war is buried deep in our evolutionary past."* Smith has examined war closely and written an unambiguous study of human nature in which he concludes that humans are *biologically wired* to fight wars. His words imply a most interesting possible answer—war is an *inherited* proclivity. Let's explore Smith's answer more fully. He tells us: "The human need for war is based on two powerful evolutionary factors: an *innate aggressiveness* born of a need to fight for food, shelter and the right to breed, *and* the

---

*While Smith's research leads him to believe that the inclination toward war is embedded in the evolutionary past of humans, a report developed by psychologists who also study war tells us that scientists do not agree violence is inherent in human biology. By inference, this means that violence is learned. This type of difference of interpretation of scientific findings is not uncommon in the history of science or social science.

human craving to belong to a group" (emphasis added).²*

This scientist has built his conclusions on the historical record that begins with primitive humans, perhaps those of the Stone Age who inhabited parts of Earth in what is academically referred to as the "dawn of history." Smith, like most academics who are uninformed about Sitchin's work, drew his conclusions based on a rationale that credits Earth's early hominids as the originators of the concept of war. This explanation implies war was born of necessity when humans reacted against threats to individual and group survival. Furthermore, Smith implies (without drawing a direct causal linkage) that early humans acted on innate emotional reactions to deadly threats. According to Sitchin's research findings, *this is not true.*

Sitchin's research does allow us to accept Smith's assertion that the proclivity to war *is inherited.* However, his research also indicates that war was *brought to Earth* by other terrestrials whose genes were impressed on humans in the process of the genetic manipulation we call "creation." Sitchin's work documents this much earlier source of the seemingly "innate" inclinations held by humans. His explanations derive from the ancient tablet sources that reveal a genetic impress placed on a Stone Age man who was *upgraded* in his developmental trajectory to make him a "willing worker." If indeed the tendency to engage in war is genetically based, then the tablet evidence tells

---

*In his book *The Most Dangerous Animal: Human Nature and the Origins of War,* Smith discusses this question: What it is about human nature that makes it possible for human beings to regularly slaughter their own kind? He tells us that the reasons why *all* human beings have the potential to be hideously cruel and destructive to one another is because we humans are our own worst enemy. While that may be true, it is not a satisfactory answer. This book is an interesting read that offers a one-sided scientist's perspective.

us that the ancient Anunnaki settlers are the carriers of the concept of war.

The historical tablet material reveals that the Nibiruans, during their eons of life on their home planet, used war and warring repeatedly. They *brought their aggressive* (and defensive) behaviors with them. What we also know for certain from tablet sources is that the technologies of warring were brought *from their home planet.* Inadvertently, Smith is correct in his findings, but he uses vague wording to describe (not explain) human tendencies, when in fact the root source of any emotional tendencies came from inhabitants of another planet.

The history of human warring behaviors is much older than Smith is aware of. What is particularly interesting is that Smith even uses the word *innate.* He would have been much more accurate if that word opened the door to his own understanding of Sitchin's findings. If he had drawn on Sitchin's research he would be able to tell us that wars on Earth first arose between factions of the other terrestrials because of animosities that originated on Nibiru. The underlying truth is that—if indeed there is a genetic source of aggressiveness—it was the genetic impress of Anunnaki genes onto the Earth-based hominid that gave rise to similar aggressive behaviors in humans.

Considering the fact that the predisposition to war seems to be exacerbated by differences between Earth-based cultures, and seems to infuse itself into human consideration as a viable problem-solving tool,* it is logical to point to a genetic source. Of course, in our historical experience, it is human decision-makers

---

*This comment does not open the discussion to the predatory behavior of many animal species who kill each other. The concept of survival of the fittest seems to apply to both humans and animals.

who decide to go to war. So it is logical to assume that these early human leaders "invented" aggressiveness manifesting as warring actions. From Sitchin's findings, we can draw a link that strongly implies that the concept of war came to Earth hundreds of thousands of years before humankind even was created.

Unfortunately, if warring is "in our genes," then we humans never may be free from the idea of war as a vehicle to effect change by using violence. One thing surely is true: if its source is learned, it would take a long and potent process of retraining for humans to move away from a dependence on war as the solution to resolving human conflicts. It might even take another genetic implant to eliminate it as a logical way of thinking if there is a genetic source. Unfortunately humans may destroy Earth as a viable habitat before such a genetic solution ever could be implemented.

War and Warring Examined

When we closely examine war and warring, we see a long list of goals that warring actions seek to accomplish. Historians tell us that nearly every recorded civilization has engaged in armed struggles, and some even exist in a constant state of war. Justifying war is a matter of identifying the benefits that accrue to the victors. However, to isolate the actual reasons for *why* war is such a prevalent feature of Earth's civilizations is a complex undertaking. It involves identifying sets of provoking circumstances and the powerful forces operating at the personal, community, sub-group, and national levels. In today's world the search for explanations of why wars are started requires that we look at those who are invested in winning outcomes, and identifying what they expect to gain. For example, a prominent explanation is that there are powerful forces that see huge economic gains going to those who benefit behind the scenes. In a religious war such as a jihad, the overt goal is domination of human minds, bodies, and behaviors that conform to the group mentality.

Typical motivations can include *revenge,* personal *jealousy,* raw territorial *aggression, repatriation* of lands and people, *taking control* of valuable resources, or *resolving or changing ideological, religious, and political differences.* War and warring are the most egregious methods that can be undertaken,* but all too often are the most used approaches. We must not forget that often wars are facilitated by powerful economic motives. Greed expressed in numerous ways contributes to decisions that lead to the waging of war. The designers and vendors of the tools of war—the weapons—of course have lots to gain, such as a market for their goods. The sale of existing technologies generates innovation directed toward making war more and more efficient. The availability of manufactured lethal weapons in the modern world makes any—or all—of these warring motivations possible. But it is not those vendors or scientists developing new weapons who are bloodied, maimed, or killed; typically it is well-meaning military volunteers and innocent people.

What we find when we look closely at the reality of modern war and warring is that this collectively sanctioned behavior is replete with all kinds of violence focused on the intention to gain control over people, territory, and resources. The primary and most used tactic to achieve warring goals is killing humans. Some groups carry out their killing goals by using the deadly force provided by face-to-face combat, or by using hand-held weapons, while others may use rocket-propelled launchers or bombs

------

*This is the opinion of this author, not one derived from any Sitchin material or other sources.

(detonated on the ground or in the air). Other groups design strategies to inflict devastation by attacking resources needed by populations—food supplies and potable water supplies.* Still others seem to engage in killing for the sake of killing.†

No matter what tactic is used, the purpose for employing any of these methods of killing is to inflict lethal damage and "to teach the enemy an emotional lesson" (if any enemy survives). An "emotional lesson" is the *threat* that if there is no capitulation, everything (human and material) will be completely destroyed. Possessions and innocent beings are the targets. Interestingly, this strategy often is designed into warring tactics, just not called out as the underlying reason.

When the goal is control over resources or to regain rightful hegemony over lands, a political leader with an army under his‡ command can amass troops and invade the desired lands, perhaps killing and maiming along the way. The nation or territory attacked is forced to either offer a defense, capitulate to occupation,

---

*Recent evidence shows that adjacent nations with long-standing disputes have threatened to reduce or cut off supplies of water for agricultural use and most importantly for use by human populations. Such a deprivation tactic makes the point that the holders of such natural resources have life-threatening power over their "enemies." See the article by Niharika Mandhana, "Water Wars: Why India and Pakistan are Squaring Off over Their Rivers," *Time,* April 16, 2012, http://content.time.com/time/world/article/0,8599,2111601,00.html.

†A typical report on the killing activities by terrorist groups can be found in the *New York Daily News* article of June 6, 2014, "Islamic Terrorist Group Releases Video and Pictures of Murderous Acts in Iraq," by Adam Edelman, Eli Rosenberg, and Joel Landau, www.nydailynews.com/news/world/islamic-terrorist-group-releases-evidence-murderous-acts-article-1.1830583.

‡Men typically lead warring efforts, but history has not forgotten the role taken by the Bible's Deborah in Israelite history and the modern use of women in combat roles.

or even engage in out and out slaughter. War can be used to eliminate those who disagree, protest, resist, or attack those in power, but it does more. It is a demoralizing set of actions set in motion to send a wider message—to instill fear, to intimidate, humiliate, terrorize, or otherwise threaten a larger population or others around the world—into capitulation to whatever the demands are. Often the true motivations for war are not overt; the actual motivations are forces acting beneath public scrutiny. These reasons are the most abhorrent because they avoid examination and rational or legal input, and often benefit only a few who hold power.

In modern wars, ingenuous tactics (in mostly remote places) have crossed the line that separates civilized from barbaric behavior.* They remind us that even more anarchic and vicious behavior is just under the surface of even modern (supposedly civilized) aggressors. Warring tactics that include use of chemicals designed for mass killing, rape of women, targeted killing of pregnant women, and forced use of children as combatants (and using girls sexually as the spoils of war), signal that civilized behavior has evaporated as the atrocities become either commonplace or sanctioned behaviors.† These are warring tactics currently used in some twenty-first century wars, which signal that even more inhumane behaviors are possible as warring continues to spread. Eventually such immoral and barbaric warring behaviors—if left uncontrolled

---

*It is likely that barbaric tactics were used in ancient and historic times, but the prevalence of such inhuman actions in modern times indicates a reverting to uncivilized approaches now outlawed by treaties, but not respected (if even known about) by lawless groups operating in remote locations. Even though repulsive, tactics such as cannibalism or beheading are being used in today's world.

†We have purposely left the destruction caused by nuclear war off this list. Complete annihilation is the intent of this type of war.

and if perpetrators are not made accountable—will destroy all of the progress made by civilizations over the past thousands of years.

Still another explanation is institutionalized warring, with its ultimate intention to carry out organized and deliberate killing of a population. It involves training selected people (often volunteers) to kill legally as members of military organizations. People can be carefully taught to kill as preparation for protecting a political territory, to carry out an ideology such as "freedom," or to carry out aggressive policies set out by an ambitious leadership. The wars of the twentieth century were motivated by leaders who sought world (or at least continental) domination. The wars of the twenty-first century are wars of extermination, perhaps fueled by a covert belief that human life no longer matters, as it no longer is precious and is easily replaceable. In other words, if human life is considered by some who promote and carry out war to have no intrinsic value, if people are not valuable and are no longer considered "children of God," then there is no hope for humanity's future.

What we know from Sitchin's research is that war and warring plagued Earth *before* humans walked its pristine landscapes. To fully understand the long trajectory of war and warring on planet Earth, we first need to look into the roots of Earth's *inhabited history*.

The Wars of
the Sumerian Tablet Records

In attempting to study the circumstances that brought the Nefilim to Earth, Sitchin mined a source known as the *Kingship in Heaven* text, which told of "lingering and bitter" struggles between two houses of Nibiruan power: the "House of Anu" and the "House of Alalu." On the planet Nibiru, ruling family relationships were of immense importance, and records were kept to trace the ancestry of those in line for power. Long lists were constructed showing genealogical records; for example, Anu's royal ancestry was traced through twenty-one ancestral couples. However, Anu's father's name was AN.SHAR.GAL, which meant "Great *Prince* of Heaven."[3] Rightful power rested with the House of Alalu, but Anu used war to gain supremacy.

There were ongoing bitter struggles between the House of Alalu and the House of Anu on Nibiru. According to Sitchin's text, this war also broke out on Earth and pitted "the gods who are in heaven" against the "gods who are upon dark-hued Earth."[4] It was called the "War of the Titans."[5] Sitchin's discussion tells us that "it had taken place in the early days of the settlement of the Nibiruans on Earth and in the aftermath of Anu's first visit to Earth . . . [and] the adversaries [were known] as 'the mighty olden gods, the gods of the olden days.'"[6]

Anu was successful in carrying out his usurpation of the throne on Nibiru, which forced the flight of Alalu to another planet.* That god's grandson, Kumarbi, began to cause trouble at the time that Anu prepared to come down to Earth to deal with the mutiny at the gold mines. In his preparations for coming to Earth, Anu decided to bring Kumarbi with him. Anu was afraid Kumarbi would stir up trouble on Nibiru in his absence; instead Kumarbi stirred up trouble on Earth. Kumarbi later conceptualized himself as the holder of supremacy on Earth and wanted to be considered "the father of all the gods." At that point, Anu decided that enough was enough. He ordered his

---

*One source indicates that Alalu came to Earth, and was the one who found gold here.

grandson, the Storm God (Teshub), to find and kill Kumarbi.*
Ferocious battles ensued. Sitchin's text tells us "in one battle
alone, no less than seventy gods participated, all riding in celestial chariots. However, Teshub prevailed."[7] So, war was the vehicle for dealing with a challenge aimed at resolving who would
have power over Earth, and also on Nibiru.

Another notable conflict that ended up in a limited war is discussed in Sitchin's work. It focused on a shady character known as
Zu, who—with cunning and inventiveness—tried to disrupt the
space operations that controlled the gold shipment missions from
Earth to Nibiru. Zu was an ambitious thug who used immoral
behavior to get what he wanted. An Anunnaki Igigi who was
assigned to the space platform monitoring duties brought Zu to
the space station where he learned about Earth's space activities.
While on the space platform, he learned the details of space operations associated with and necessary to the gold transshipment
processes. Then when he came down to Earth, Zu ingratiated
himself with Enlil (through lies and false behavior that somehow
prompted Enlil's trust), even after Enki warned Enlil to be wary.

When Enlil stepped away from the room where the Tablets of
Destiny (which controlled space operations) were held, Zu seized
those extremely valuable objects that controlled essential functions
and took off in a "Sky Chamber" to hide and defend himself in the
mountains. It was Ninurta, Enlil's foremost son, who had the courage to step up and fight Zu. Using vehicles known as "Whirlwind
Birds," Ninurta successfully defeated the renegade who was captured, brought to trial, convicted, and sentenced to death.[8] The
Tablets of Destiny then were re-installed in their proper place.

---

*Obviously the king held the power of life and/or death over those who were
at cross-purposes with him.

These two battles were notable events in the first several thousands of years of Anunnaki life on Earth. While they may have been among the first battles on the earthly planet, they were not the last.

Subsequent Wars on Earth

The ancient texts tell of two wars known as the Pyramid Wars, which were the first Earth-based wars that used humans as combatants. Both of these conflicts were carried out after the Deluge.

The First Pyramid War had its roots in the struggle over control of the space facilities and over Earth itself. The first battles took place in Upper Egypt. Horus, the son of Isis and Osiris, established a metal foundry at Edfu located south of Karnak on the Nile. At this site, weapons referred to as "divine iron" were forged. There Horus trained an army of Metal People who carried a "harpoon-like" weapon. Sitchin tells us that this was an army of *humans*, "the first men ever to have been armed by the gods . . . the first men to have been enlisted by a god to fight in the wars *between* the gods."[9] The god who accompanied this army was Ra/Marduk (Enki's foremost son known as a troublemaker), who traveled, observed, and fought from the sky in his "Boat of Heaven."

Together, gods and men fought several battles, and after vanquishing the enemy who hid in the waters east of Egypt, finally Marduk/Ra said: "Let this place be known as the place where thine victory in the southlands has been established."[10] The victories of Horus were complete as he fought off enemies from the skies, on land, and in the waters. Battles were fought from Nubia to Syene (Aswan) and from Thebes to Dendera. Forces were under the command of Seth, brother of Osirus. These were the places where great temples were built years later. In this war Horus adopted a notable symbol as his emblem—the Winged Disk.*

Then the battleground shifted to the chain of lakes east of Egypt proper, which separated Egypt from the Sinai, the lands of Seth. Several battles between Horus and Seth were fought on land and in the air. It was "god-to-god" combat. In the recorded works of scholar E. A. Wallis Budge, he indicates that this was not only the first battle to involve men in war among gods, but the victories were the result of the weapons made of iron.[11] According to Egyptian writings, *this was the time when "man learned to lift sword against man."*[12]

The Second Pyramid War was carried out as a contest over who would have control of the Great Pyramid at Giza. Sitchin's text tells us that whoever controlled "the Great Pyramid and its companions at Giza, shared in the control of the space activities, of the comings and goings of the gods, [and] of the vital supply link to and from the Twelfth Planet."[13]

Horus advanced northward from the southern uplands toward the site of the pyramids. After one difficult battle, Seth was banished to the Asiatic lands. A new mission control center had to be developed after the Deluge, and Jerusalem was selected as the site of this important space facility. It was located in the lands of Shem, lands allotted to Enlil-ites, but it ended up under the illegal control of the line of Enki. Sitchin points out that it was Ninurta (Enlil's foremost son) and Marduk (Enki's firstborn son) who were leaders of the opposing camps in this war. Clearly this was a war to regain rightful occupation of previously assigned lands, and specifically, of Jerusalem. Marduk, as an Enki-ite, was

---

*This symbol has come to be closely identified with all things Anunnaki.

the "enemy" whose clan had illegally settled the lands "belonging" to Enlil's progeny.

From what the tablets tell us about the tactics used in this war we learn of weapons that will ring an eerie death knell to our modern ears. Not only did Ninurta use his "Divine Brilliant Weapon"*and his "Divine Storm Bird," but some additional weapons were also brought to bear. Here, in Sitchin's words, we learn the gruesome story of what these weapons accomplished:

> Under this onslaught, the Enemy forces kept retreating south. It was then that the war assumed its ferocious and vicious character, when Ninurta lead the Enlilite gods in an attack on the heartland of Nergal's African domain and his temple-city, Meslam. They scorched the earth and made the rivers run red with the blood of the innocent bystanders—men, women, and children of the Abzu.[14]

For launching this battle, Ninurta earned, we are told, the title "Vanquisher of Meslam." In these battles the attackers resorted to the use of chemical warfare. We read that Ninurta "rained on the city poison-bearing missiles," which "he catapulted into it; the poison, by itself, destroyed the city."[15] In a tablet text we also read of another weapon used by Ninurta that, like a modern flamethrower, blasted propelled fire upon the mountains. This weapon is referred to in the phrase "the godly Weapon of the Gods, whose Tooth is bitter, smote down the people."[16] Likely it was a flamethrower. The tablet words paint a gruesome picture:

---

*Likely this was a laser-type weapon (or possibly a nuclear weapon), a deduction we make because of the damage it caused to human flesh and organs.

The Weapon which Tears Apart
robbed the senses;
The Tooth skinned them off.
Tearing-apart he stretched upon the land;
The canals he filled with blood,
in the Enemyland for dogs like milk to lick.[17]

Sitchin continues by telling us that Marduk (also known as Azag) called on the defenders to show *no more* resistance. Ninurta took this lack of resistance as a sign of victory. After another attack, Ninurta "burst out in a song of victory." He proclaimed himself the "lord of the high mountains," and went further to boast that "of the mountains which to horizon raise their peaks. In the mountains, I am the master."[18]

These words set out a barbaric display of war tactics that were being implemented for the first time, at least considering what we know. The vicious actions were part of the "practice of war" that this second-generation "god" was able to legitimately employ. It was a winner-takes-all battle, with no regard for life, limb, or human consequences. There was no moral code yet developed—or even conceived of—to guide and shape civilized war and warring behavior at the time of this Second Pyramid War.

With this picture in our minds, we can understand how the leaders who conduct modern warfare have an ancient model for assaulting their own populations and using on enemies. A modern replica of this kind of no-holds-barred warfare has taken place in the same part of the world as the ancient ones took place.* There

---

*We refer here to the 2013 events of the Syrian civil war launched by an entrenched leader who used chemical weapons on a portion of his own population. Ironically, the country of Syria is only a couple of hundred miles from Giza where the Pyramid War battles took place.

is an eerie similarity to the delivery system by which the Syrian government used rockets to catapult nerve gas into the residential area of a sleeping population in a Bagdad suburb. It is almost as though the leaders in Syria had these tablets in hand and were reading from them as though from a script. Hopefully, the world has changed enough since ancient times to bring judgment to bear on such modern barbarism and hold the perpetrators accountable for these war crimes. Regardless of how the modern leader obtained his ideas, a moral world should extract some form of accountability from him and those around him for inflicting such atrocious actions as part of his war.

Modern Wars

History is replete with examples of one war followed by another over the last two thousand years. The historical record shows that humans have an almost "irresistible" inclination to engage in war—with or without any political attempts to avoid it. Historians tell us that wars are some of the most studied, detailed, and tarnished periods of human history, with the associated killing, maiming, and material destruction taking on the same characteristics as those carried out by the ancient "gods."

The twentieth century alone witnessed numerous wars that exacted huge tolls of human life: two World Wars (with the word "world" an exaggeration); a war to halt territorial aggression (the Korean War); a war to rid a country of colonialism and prevent the expansion of communism (the Vietnam War); a war to reclaim lands once bequeathed by the Israelite God to the Jews (the 1967 war between Israel and Egypt); various tribal and territorial wars between countries in Africa; the Iraq-Iran territorial struggle over oil resources; two Iraqi wars to rid that country of a dictator and protect oil supplies; a war in Afghanistan to protect the population from religious tyrants; a war in Somalia to rid the country of corrupt warlords; and the brutal and immoral civil war inside the country of Syria (that is expanding and involving territory east of Syria's borders). This list is not in any way an exhaustive one. However, it highlights those wars of the twentieth century that carried high death tolls.

Modern wars seem to use similar destructive weapons to those used by the ancient "gods": huge cannons mounted on tanks (or airplanes) to increase protected mobility and a longer range of killing; flamethrowers; laser weapons; and bombs of all types to create explosive havoc. This list does not even mention air and sea firepower capabilities to facilitate war and increase the killing of those who are labeled as the enemy, and which take the lives of any human in the line of fire.

The proclivity to use war to achieve the numerous quests for power, whether in modern or ancient times, answers one of our opening questions: How can humans justify using war to achieve their power-hungry and killing goals? The simple answer is: *humans cannot justify the use of war.*

There is no easy answer to the question: Why do humans look to war to resolve various territorial, political, or personal disputes? While personal disputes have almost disappeared as a cause for large-scale war,* wars between nations for control over resources still exist.

---

*The type of war such as that carried out for generations between the Hatfield and McCoy clans no longer occurs, at least to the same degree as it did in those mountains of the eastern United States. Such disputes now typically are handled in the courts. However, killing on a personal level, such as killing to fulfill a vendetta, does still happen, especially when the dispute is between "families" where this sort of retribution has occurred for generations.

Wars to relieve oppression and to render "payback" for gross injustices against regimes and populations may still be provoked in the future. Wars to establish new territories (or even nations) to accomplish religious goals are emerging. In other words, war will be used to accomplish human striving for purposes we have described (above) and those not yet identified. It seems from a review of the evidence of modern times that war is endemic among leaders of the human inhabitants of Earth. We can go further by saying that war is a pervasive characteristic of humanity, probably inherited from our ancient ancestors.

What is blatantly clear is that war has its roots buried deeper than the existence of humans on this planet. The phenomenon of war was born on another planet, and bequeathed to humans as a negative gift from the gods by genetic means. Only future civilizations smart enough to overcome the deep-rooted ancient proclivities can rid Earth of wars. This is a sad conclusion, but unfortunately a true one. If we return to the question posed in the title of this chapter, the answer is "yes and no." Yes, humans have absorbed the use of war, but no, war was not invented by humans—they inherited it.

Sitchin's belief that what happened in the past foretells what will happen in the future indicates that a nuclear holocaust will take place in the Near East in the not too distant future. If that takes place, it may remove any future concept of war on Earth, and take humanity with it. An ancient nuclear holocaust did occur on the Sinai Peninsula in 2024 BCE. A close review of this ancient event prompts a most compelling question: On whose side were those who authorized the use of weapons of mass destruction—those with the intent to continue killing earthlings, or those trying to save them? We will explore this question in the next chapter, and reveal a very interesting and provocative answer.

7

Armageddon—
Global Catastrophe?

The next war will be fought with atom bombs
and the one after that
with spears.

HAROLD UREY*

Armageddon is not the end of the world.
It's a gathering place for enormous armies.
God's summons for deceived human leaders
to enter into a decisive battle
with Him at Jerusalem.

JEROLD AUST†

---

*Harold Urey (1893–1981) was a physical chemist who played a significant role in the development of the atom bomb. He received the Nobel Prize for Chemistry in 1934 for his discovery of deuterium, and held prestigious faculty positions throughout his career as a scientist.
†Jerold Aust is a United Church of God pastor, a writer and editor of *The Good News* magazine, and teacher of Speech Communication for UCG's ministerial online program (www.ucg.org).

What does the word *Armageddon* mean? Surveying several definitions gives us an array of opinions to consider. In today's world this word raises the specter of nuclear disaster, as scientist Harold Urey points out in the first epigraph to this chapter. However, other experts tell us that this word brings forward a range of both positive and negative definitions, and also carries several implications for inquiring minds to ponder. Some religiously oriented views refer to Armageddon as the "Coming of the Day of the Lord," or the time of the "second coming of Christ." Using a more somber tone, many have come to believe that this word refers to "the confrontation of Evil (Satan)" with the "forces of Good" (God and Jesus). Conversely, still others hold that Armageddon will be the time of the "annihilation of Earth as we know it," a "Doomsday." That is the implication of Urey, who predicts that after the *next* war, all that will be left as usable weapons will be spears.

A hopeful perspective is advanced by Jerold Aust (also cited on the previous page) who gives us a reassuring opinion: "Armageddon is *not* the end of the world. It is a gathering place." In his Internet piece, Aust ends his discussion of perspectives focused on commonly quoted negative views with encouraging excerpts defining Armageddon as "God's war."

> Armageddon, or Har–Magedon, is a transliteration of the Greek equivalent of the Hebrew expression Har Meghid·dohn meaning "Mountain of Megiddo," or "Mountain of Assembly of Troops." It is linked with "the war of the great day of God the Almighty." So Armageddon is not a political skirmish, an economic disaster, a nuclear holocaust, or a human conflict. Rather, Armageddon is God's war.[1]

The references to the Israeli settlement of Megiddo and its nearby plains most likely are drawn from an ancient prophesy with respect to a coming intervention by God himself. Armageddon in this context means that:

> The last great battle of man's age will take place in the nation of Israel. The armies will gather at a place the Bible calls Armageddon. So, not surprisingly, Armageddon has come to portray our worst nightmare: the end of the world. A more detailed speculation speaks of it as a battle of cataclysmic proportions, possibly a *nuclear war* that will annihilate mankind.[2]

What this explanation emphasizes is that what will happen when Armageddon is on the horizon will not be directed by decisions made by humankind; rather, it will be a "great day of God." These differing perspectives leave us with an array of possibilities to consider. Those who live by faith will take heart; those who hold pessimistic mindsets will—without doubt—draw more ominous conclusions.

The Near East Focus, Modern and Ancient

If we look at a commonly referenced Internet site[3] we find a brief discussion dealing with Armageddon that resonates with some of the current situations that require us to consider the climate of negative change—religious and political—occurring across the Near East. Sitchin adds yet another perspective on the definition of Armageddon, one based on his research and mastery of biblical and ancient history. He tells us that the Dead Sea scroll collection contains a long and dramatic discussion* of a future "Final War," which will pit "The Sons of Light against the Sons of Darkness."[4] In Sitchin's interpretation of these words, "[Armageddon] envisages spreading warfare—local battles that will first involve Judea's immediate neighbors, which shall increase in ferocity and scope until the whole ancient world [is] engulfed."[5]

This was the threat faced by the Essenes a few thousand years ago, but if we read it as a farsighted future prediction, it forces us to remember the array of threats that have been leveled for years against Israel by all of its Arab neighbors, and compels us also to factor in the radical religious and political discontent that has spread across North Africa (and other parts of Africa) and around the Near East in the first few decades of the twenty-first century.

Another situation, carrying an even more ominous threat, comes from Iran's pursuit of its goal to accumulate enriched uranium. Successful development of that capability poses a serious threat to Near East peace, and brings the specter of nuclear war as a possible reality to consider in the foreseeable future. Israel's articulate leaders are particularly wary of Iran's public words, warning the Western world that deceit is a viable strategy in a politically charged covert war. Iran's continued insistence that it will keep refining uranium (ostensibly for peaceful uses) and that they have a right to nuclear capability is a veiled threat. Regardless of the larger world's efforts to negotiate a stoppage of Iran's efforts to refine uranium, Iran continues to boldly focus its determined rhetoric toward its goal. This incongruity lends itself to fears that a future filled with an ominous threat does indeed exist, and if

---

*This refers to the War Scroll, the longest document in the Dead Sea Scroll collection, and an unusual one in that it was etched on a sheet of copper, which was then rolled. To open it, it had to be cut into segments.

carried out in the way the critics fear, a dire outcome is inevitable.

Some predict that Jerusalem is the focus of a future disastrous event. We are reminded that Jerusalem held a position of central importance in ancient times. In minds steeped in history, even the mention of Jerusalem as a focus is a warning. Taking this information seriously, and factoring in sectarian violence in the Near East areas, the doomsday explanations of what Armageddon might mean point to the conclusion that *something ominous is on the horizon and it is focused on Israel, Iran, and the entire Near East.*

Another factor to keep in mind is that it was the ancient Nefilim leaders who wanted to keep the Sinai spaceport from a boastful Nefilim who articulated his objective to take control of it. As will be apparent in our retelling of the story below, those who were in the role of the protectors of the Nefilim linkages with their home planet *used the nuclear option* to *stop* their opponent, Marduk, the ambitious braggart. Then, in 1945 the American leadership saw the nuclear option as the only way to *stop* the Japanese warring in the Pacific. In other words, in the two examples of use of nuclear weapons on Earth in the past, *it was the "good guys" who used nuclear weapons.* Similarly, it may be the *opponents* of the belligerent parties who resort to use of nuclear technology in the future, not the ones doing the shouting and terrorizing. This is an outcome worth close scrutiny.

Zecharia Sitchin's belief that the past predicts the future was never more clear than in his book, *The End of Days,* where he confirmed his certainty about the relationship between history, the present, and the future with these bold words: "The Present stems from the Past; the Past is the Future."[6] Further, it was Sitchin's contention that time was circular, and that what happened in the past foretells what *will happen* in the future. It was his long-held opinion that the catastrophe that occurred in ancient times would be repeated. If we accept Sitchin's belief,* then 2024 CE holds a long predicted disastrous event that the world must be reminded of, prepared for, but committed to averting by every means conceivable.

Sitchin's view, as he clearly states it in *The End of Days* on page 281 and thereafter, is that the "risk of a nuclear threat hangs over the very same historical place [where it first occurred—the Sinai]. It is enough reason to ask: Will history repeat itself—does history repeat itself in some mysterious way, every twenty-one centuries?" We would do well to heed his prophecy, based as it is on historical facts. To understand his future prediction, we need to look at the historical circumstances that produced the ancient—first—nuclear event of 2024 BCE. Unfortunately, it is little known to modern readers and audiences. *One of Sitchin's most poignant contributions is to remind us of this piece of nuclear history and to alert us to its possible repeat occurrence.*

The Past—The Ancient Nuclear Event

What circumstances existed in ancient times that provoked the ominous decision to deploy and detonate nuclear weapons? What state of affairs was so dire that it elicited such drastic action? Sitchin tells us the entire saga, using the *Erra Epic* as his tablet source.†

The provoking problem stemmed from the fact that when

---

*As Sitchin devoted his life to the study of far ancient history, and considering the scope and depth of his base of knowledge, we have a good foundation upon which to *accept* his belief.

†A translation of this Sumerian record can be found at www.bibliotecapleyades.net/sitchin/erra_epic.htm

Enki's firstborn son, Marduk, emerged from his seventy-two year exile, he renewed his long-standing ambition to take the city of Babylon, with the intent of gaining supremacy over the whole of Sumer. Even more provocatively, he vowed to take control of the spaceport located in the Sinai. Sitchin tells us: "Control of the site of the . . . spaceport was tantamount to control of the links between Earth and Nibiru."[7] Securing that vital site and preventing Marduk's intended control was what provoked the use of nuclear weapons.

A penetrating analysis of several circumstances in motion at that time allows us to build an understanding of the full saga as it unfolded. Marduk's son, Nabu, had been roaming Canaan's settlements gaining supremacy and adherents. Sitchin's text tells us that "the whole land of Moab had come under Nabu's influence."[8] Then an Enlil-ite invasion of Sinai came from the east, using the route known as the "Way of the Kings," an inland route on the east of the Jordan River. The Enlil-ite forces moved south with the intention of taking control of a crossroad oasis in that wilderness in order to reach their intended destination, a goal that never was completed. A small city called El-Paran was the expected target of the invaders, but they were beaten back at Ein Mishpat, a place also known as Kadesh-Barnea.

The kings of the Canaanite cities of Sodom, Gomorrah, Admah, Zebi'im, and Zoar (all cities located along a valley south and east of the Dead Sea) came forward to engage in battle, but they turned back when their route was blocked by an army of horsemen.[9] Why did horse-riding "invaders" want to reach a destination such as the fortified oasis of Nakhl in the central plain of Sinai, a desolate place in the middle of a formidable desert? Sitchin alone asks a critical question: *who blocked the invaders,* forcing them to turn back? His research gave him the answer. It was the biblical patriarch, Abraham. But why would Abraham and his elite troops have done that? Sitchin's text tells us this:

> There have been no answers; and no answers can make sense except the ones offered by us [Sitchin]: The only significance of the destination was its Spaceport, and the one who blocked the advance at Kadesh-Barnea was Abraham. From earlier times Kadesh-Barnea was the closest place where men could approach in the region of the Spaceport without special permission.[10]

This "almost" war had for its (underlying) main purpose "to prevent the return of Marduk and to thwart the efforts of Nabu from gaining access to the spaceport."[11] The records indicate that Ninurta (Enlil's son) had control of Babylon, the city Marduk intended to—and did eventually—take over. Most important to this situation is to understand that Nergal (Enki's son) and Ninurta considered Marduk's assertions (that he intended to control the spaceport) to be *real* warnings. To address those threats, Nergal confronted his father (Enki) in a prolonged argument, essentially imploring Enki to realize that Marduk seriously meant to take control of the spaceport. Nergal pleaded with his father to prevent this *at all cost.*

The *Erra Epic* tells us that Nergal had devised an ominous plan to deal with Marduk and his son, Nabu, to be used *if no other solution* was proffered. Nergal's plan was to permanently thwart Marduk's intentions by taking drastic action. With no hesitation about taking matters into his own hands, Nergal vowed he would unleash the Ultimate Weapons, the tablet designation for "nuclear weapons." As recorded on one of the tablets, Nergal stated that he clearly understood that "such an extreme measure [on his part] was not taken lightly."[12]

The great gods sat in continuous Council of War, and in constant communication with the king, Anu, who remained on Nibiru throughout the time this entire situation was under consideration. Anu urged one more encounter between Nergal and Marduk be undertaken to try to convince Marduk to leave Babylon—but even that strong persuasion did not meet with success. Marduk was stubbornly, and perhaps even fanatically, resolute. Enki, much to Nergal's surprise, supported Marduk, his firstborn. As Nergal argued the seriousness of this case to his father, Enki became so enraged with him that he banished him from his presence.[13]

Nergal left that acrimonious discussion in a huff, with an even stronger determination to put his plan into effect. Sitchin recounts the words of Nergal as he announced his intent, as recorded on a tablet:

> *The lands I will destroy, to a dust-heap make*
> *   them;*
> *the cities I will upheaval,*
> *to desolation turn them;*
> *the mountains I will flatten, their animals*
> *   make disappear;*
> *the seas I will agitate, that which teems in*
> *   them I will decimate;*
> *the people I will make vanish, their souls shall*
> *   turn to vapor;*
> *none shall be spared.*[14]

With Anu's permission given to go ahead with the plan, Ninurta traveled in his Divine Black Bird (likely a fighter plane) to the Lower World (meaning Africa) to find that Nergal had begun the process of priming the nuclear weapons. Ninurta made it very clear to Nergal that these "weapons of mass destruction"* were to be used *only* against the sites approved by Anu and the Council. Apparently both Anu and Enlil approved these amended dimensions of Nergal's plan. Also, those authorities insisted that warnings be given to the Igigi on the space platform of the upcoming explosive events.

Nergal finally agreed, although reluctantly, to follow these limiting directives by using *precision bombing* (Sitchin's words were "selective targeting") to avoid any indiscriminate destruction to Anunnaki sites, or to the seas, and he also agreed to leave the area north of Sumer (Mesopotamia) out of the attack. But Nergal also indicated that he wanted to be sure that the place of hiding of Marduk's son, Nabu, was destroyed, and that the spaceport operations center that was located underground in a nearby mountain (the place from where spaceport operations were controlled), was *inside* the zone of destruction.

Nergal and Ninurta then journeyed to the Sinai, armed with the weapons. Ninurta had decided to hit the spaceport as the first detonation site. Tablets record his actions with this description:

> *The Awesome Seven [weapons] without parallel,*
> *trailed behind him.*

---

*This often-used and therefore recognizable phrase is our deliberate attempt to draw out the similarity of the ancient event to our modern situation.

At the Mount Most Supreme [the name of the
control center]
the hero arrived;
He raised his hand—
the mount was smashed;
The plain by the Mount Most Supreme [runways]
he then obliterated;
In its forest not a tree-stem was left standing.[15]

The feat Ninurta carried out was historically significant, yet highly destructive. Next, it was Nergal's turn to seek vengeance. He guided himself up the King's Highway (the inland route from Egypt to the north). "The cities he finished off, to desolation he overturned them. In the mountains he caused starvation, their animals he made perish."[16] The neck of land that separated the lower plain from the main body of the Dead Sea waters was destroyed by the concussion of the detonations, allowing the plain to flood with Dead Sea water. This inundation took the sinful cities of Sodom and Gomorrah *off the map,* and left the southern extension of the Dead Sea in its place. All life in those waters was eliminated by the radiation produced by those weapons.

Sitchin tells us that neither the nuclear blasts nor their brilliant flashes were felt or seen in Sumer in 2024 BCE, but the nuclear event did have a profound effect on that entire area, and well beyond. In his final book he documents the Sinai event with NASA aerial photographic evidence.[17] The scorched and blackened (shallow) crater stands out in the photo in contrast with the white limestone uplands around it.

Sitchin begins the chapter that lays out all of these details by retelling the biblical story of Abraham and Lot (his nephew).* They were visited by three "beings" who seemed to "just appear" out of nowhere. When both Abraham and Lot met the three "men" (each meeting occurred in a separate setting), they recognized two as Mal'akkim (emissaries) and the third as "the Lord."†

The purpose of these encounters was to forewarn Abraham and Lot of the decision to destroy Sodom because of the immoral proclivities of the population there. The three "men" were on a reconnaissance mission to determine if the reports of the sinfulness of the people of the two cities, Sodom and Gomorrah, indeed were true—and they did find the information to be truthful. Lot, his two daughters, and his wife, were directed to go to the mountains to avoid what was to become the blast and its shock wave. Abraham, who was camped in the mountains overlooking the Dead Sea, also was instructed to move west to avoid the fallout. The biblical story tells that Lot's wife, disobeying the warning, turned to look back at the city as the family group hurried south, and as a result of this defiance, was *consumed* by the heat wave of the blast, which turned her into a cloud of vapor—not salt.‡

---

*Chapter 14, "The Nuclear Holocaust," of *The Wars of Gods and Men* explains what happened and who the players were.

†The story is vague as to exactly who "the lord" is—leaving it to Sitchin to interpret him to be Yahweh. In Sitchin's book *Divine Encounters,* he explores all the possibilities as to who, of all the possible personages, Yahweh could be, eliminating them one by one in his discussion.

‡Sitchin includes a long footnote in *The Wars of Gods and Men* (313–314), in which he gives his expert assessment of the translated word used to explain what happened to Lot's wife, and how it was mistakenly translated to imply she turned to "salt," when, in fact, it means she became "vapor," likely from the nuclear heat and wind of the blast.

These events indeed comprised a disaster with widespread consequences. In addition to the blast effects, spatially extensive *desolation** was produced by a dense fallout cloud that spread from the blast site (in central Sinai) eastward across the northern part of the Arabian Peninsula's Nafud desert, then along the thirtieth parallel to Sumer. The Sumerian tablet records refer to this contaminated atmospheric anomaly as an Evil Wind (see appendix B) that drifted from west to east.

After that radiation cloud passed through, Sumer was no more. The buildings stood, but no life of any kind remained. What a terrible end to a glorious place that was the birthplace of all habitation at the time of the original settlement of Earth.† To this day, the levels of radiation found in the ground water of this region are high enough to cause human reproductive problems for long-time users of those water sources, meaning for settlers who now live in the area.‡

The lesson here for modern times is that everything humanly possible must be done to prevent a repeat of such a tragic nuclear event. What is important is for modern humans to give serious attention to those circumstances currently in motion that threaten a repeat of this devastating historical event. Humankind

---

*The word used in the tablet records that was translated as "desolation" means "complete destruction of all life."
†Sitchin devotes several pages (334–342) of his book, *The Wars of Gods and Men,* to the lamentations over the desolation of the Sumerian settlements by the aftermath of this nuclear explosion.
‡My earlier book, *The Legacy of Zecharia Sitchin* (104–105), includes a report of rock samples retrieved by a participant in a Sitchin tour group visiting the Sinai, which were examined later by scientists and found to contain the rare and pure isotope U-235. Those experts concluded that the presence of that isotope "could *only* have resulted from purification not yet achieved on Earth by modern technology" and therefore came from a nuclear explosion.

must seriously consider Sitchin's most provocative contribution— the warning that history repeats itself.

The Future—The Predicted Nuclear Event

The previous discussion explains the provoking reasons behind the ancient nuclear event and the devastating results. Now we turn our attention to a future event that, if Sitchin is correct, will occur in (or around) 2024 CE. First, we should ask this question: are there factors operating in the beginning of the twenty-first century that would allow such a future prediction to hold *any* validity? Unfortunately, the answer to this question is "yes." There are ominous signs in the larger Near Eastern region that suggest that such an event is possible.

For example, there again are acrimonious nations (and terrorist groups) who have publically vowed to annihilate Israel. Beginning in the latter part of the twentieth century, the countries of Iran and Libya undertook nuclear development. Libya had a twenty-year-long slate of activities focused on that goal throughout the 1980s that did not progress to a weapons level, primarily due to that country's inability to obtain the necessary equipment from numerous commercial sources located in several places around the world. At present (2014), the Libyan nuclear program has been all but dismantled under the supervision of the International Atomic Energy Agency (IAEA), and it either remains at an initial stage, or indeed is disbanded.

Of continued concern is Libya's chemical weapons stockpiles (particularly mustard blister agents loaded in artillery rounds) that, as of the negotiated deadline of September 2013, *had not yet been destroyed.* Intelligence sources indicate that some (or even all) of these chemical weapons have "disappeared" (likely stolen) from unguarded arsenals, removed (it is thought), by Al Qaeda in the Islamic Maghreb.[18] These chemical weapons could emerge as a threat to Near East populations in the future if indeed they are in the hands of this (or another) terrorist group.

Iran is the nation that has provoked the most serious nuclear threat, one that has alarmed its regional neighbors. In mid-summer of 2013, Iran's foreign policy appeared to soften when its newly elected prime minister began discussions to open the door to Iran's "supposed change of intention" relative to producing nuclear weapons. This official of Iran's government repeatedly said Iran does not (and never did) have the intention to develop nuclear weapons. Under a previous prime minister, Iran's position had adhered to a hard-line no-compromise approach and the then official spokesperson stated that whatever processes were in motion would continue. Because of increasing hardships on Iran's population caused by sanctions previously imposed (when Iran first started a nuclear development program), the people, and now the government, want the sanctions lifted. The new prime minister was allowed to state publically that that nation's nuclear intentions were for peaceful uses only (i.e., power generation).

Some strong voices from Western countries continue to urge the world powers to continue the sanctions in order to force Iran to completely cease and desist in its uranium enrichment program. To continue to run the centrifuges (the technology that is key to the enrichment, meaning to make U-235 by freeing three neutrons from the U-238) was considered by the critics to leave Iran with the ability to shift its enrichment capability into weapons production quickly. Initially Iran agreed, but as negotiations progressed, they announced they would continue with the enrichment process. This decision on Iran's part was considered a dangerous "hedge" and alerted regional critics to continue their strong objections and globally focused warnings.

Iran's neighbors in the Near East region have raised serious doubts that the publicized intention to cooperate in negotiations is an honest one. The presumption is that Iran's covert intention is to produce bombs "at all cost." Iran still has a nuclear facility for use in the refinement, processing, and storage facilities for raw uranium. It also has facilities building rocket delivery systems that can be armed with nuclear devices.

Iran is not the only problem nation in the Near East. The country of Syria has a seemingly intractable problem, primarily focused on chemical weapons. In 2013 the national army was accused of using saran gas on a portion of Bagdad's suburban population. The government denies culpability, and accuses the rebels fighting against the political regime of this reprehensible act. While subsequently agreeing to allow experts from an international chemical weapons organization to *inventory and destroy* all Syria's stockpiles (activity undertaken in the fall of 2013), accusations have been floated that the government *did not identify all the locations* where these weapons were stockpiled, and that Syria's government moved some stockpiles out of the country (most likely to Iraq). If true, a chemical weapons threat still exists in this region where civil war has raged for well over four years.

These perspectives also bring a considerably larger, more spatially extensive threat to the fore as a "plague" of Islamic jihadist unrest grows across the entire Near Eastern region and continues to envelop more and more nations. A conservative fundamentalist mentality fuels this threat and reveals an undercurrent of *radical* Islam that feeds the erupting fires of political as well as sectarian protests, and intensifies public discontent. Such unrest is ripe for corruption by powerful voices from religious fanatics, perhaps setting the stage for a potential future war to achieve a jihadist revolution. Adherents to radical Islamic views abhor Western influences on their populations. This is the religious and political undercurrent that is described by an informed source as a "cultural social ideology dominating all aspects of life." More specifically, this view states

> They have a primary objective to dominate all those within its reach and suppress all other ideologies, movements, and beliefs in its path. [It] *is dedicated to the conquest of the world, by any means possible. . . .* Terrorism is only one of the tactics used by radicals, with new tactics arising every day (emphasis added).[19]

These religious and political forces have all the symptoms of a contagious infection. The minds adhering to these beliefs defy rational thought and logical ways of conceptualizing and expressing alternatives. Some believe this movement is based in an emotionally defined ideology that is a corrupted interpretation of its original authority, the Koran. The intent of the several radical Islamist groups who have secured control of numerous settlements in northern Syria and beyond, for example, argue that they are a separate Islamic *state* that follows fundamental beliefs and strict practices known as "sharia law." Already they are promulgating a name for their controlled territory, calling itself the "Islamic State of Iraq and Syria (or Levant)" (ISIS or ISIL). Known to be comprised of terrorist adherents from several parts of the Islamic world, they have—so far—targeted Christian residents for annihilation. Who is next? Massacres of huge numbers of long-standing Christian communities already have been documented, according to a report filed by

Nour Malas for the *Middle East News* service on February 27, 2013. The adherents to these radical Islamist beliefs have captured minds from groups—and radicalized individuals—in Tunisia, Libya, Iraq, Britain, and Chechen regions of Russia (and perhaps other parts of the Islamic world as well).

The geographic scope of these groups, now coalescing in a multi-state area, is foreboding and adds fuel to Sitchin's prediction that a repeat nuclear event is possible. With widespread unrest growing more pervasive and powerful by the year, it does seem likely it will build toward a violent eruption in the near future. *The opponents of this radical movement may see a nuclear option as the only way to stop its growth.* These data and discussions lay out the continued threats that are "alive and well" in the region. With all these provocative activities and new ones that could emerge at any time, the prophecy still is completely valid. If the Sitchin prediction comes true, the powerful nations of the world will have failed to rise to the preventive challenge needed to avoid disaster; the world as we know it will no longer exist to consider alternatives.

We repeat the admonition stated previously: with the known threats, the *world's population must be reminded of, prepared for, but encouraged to work to avert nuclear weapon use by every means conceivable. Armageddon, defined as "doomsday," must be avoided at all cost.*

Future Studies: Assessing the Possible, Probable, and Plausible

How can the future and threats intended for the future be assessed? Certainly we cannot just assert a future scenario without evidence and just causes. Luckily, we can gain some support for thinking seriously about future scenarios by drawing on a *field of study that provides a methodology* for assessing trajectories that already are in motion. The academic discipline of future studies can provide us with a methodology for consideration. It involves continuously projecting forward on a timeline that assumes a unity of reality, based on an identifiable "chunk" of time, and using thoughts and conjectures as tools of thought—not predictions or conclusions.

Projecting from the *known* to the *unknown* is not a matter of setting out an ungrounded supposition. *Credible futures thinking involves looking at facts already known in order to identify logical progressions across time.* The futures arena considers four types of outcomes: *possible, probable, preferable,* and *plausible.* We can shorten this list by eliminating the *preferable* option. It would be "preferable" to not have to deal with the idea of a nuclear event, no matter what the provoking circumstances. Drawing on the work of futurist Norman Henchy, we now will consider three types of futures: *possible* futures consisting of *what may be; probable* futures dealing with *what will likely be;* and *plausible* futures that give attention to *what could be.*[20]

The existing threats for the use of nuclear weapons fall into the category of "what may be" possible. According to some vocal politically astute individuals in Israel, the nuclear *possibility* is a real one. It is important to emphasize that such an event can arise from aggressors, but also can be used in a limited way as a deterrent by friendly forces (as in the ancient and historic past).

To assess the *probable* futures that have been laid out here regarding "what will likely be," would cross the line into a prediction. While futures analyses are *not* predictions, we must ask: Is there a likelihood of a nuclear event? The answer clearly is "yes."

A nuclear event, based on the evidence we have set out, is *plausible*. If we consider this as an option, given the evidence available as of the end of 2014, a strong indication points to the fact that Iran could have a capability that could put in motion their long-standing threat to "wipe Israel off the map." Cultural factors fuel Iran's statements and could stem from their aggressive past history of war and territorial conquests. However, all that can be said from the evidence currently in hand is that Iran's intent to become a nuclear power could be based on following through on their persistent and often repeated threats.

In futures discussions, John Peterson's work stands out as notable. In his book *Out of the Blue: How to Anticipate Wild Cards and Big Future Surprises,* he introduces the notion of unexpected, unanticipated events and processes he calls "wild cards." In the complex arena of the Near East, "wild cards" complicate the analysis of threats but are well worth keeping in mind.

In the final analysis, all we can draw on is Sitchin's published prediction, based as it is on his belief that there are extremely long cycles that have been shown to produce repeating events. Sitchin's statements clearly were "predictions," which do not adhere to the futures disciplinary methodology. Given that he never called himself a futurist, we can allow him the prerogative to set out a future scenario (based on his thorough research efforts). In closing it is worth repeating an emphasis already set out in this discussion: the world would do well to *know about* Sitchin's prediction and the basis on which he makes it, and *work to avoid at all cost a "modern-day Armageddon."*

The Past
Informs the Future

The historical sense involves a perception,
not only of the pastness of the past,
but of its presence.
Time present and time past are
both perhaps present in time future,
and time future is contained in time past.

T. S. ELIOT, *FOUR QUARTETS*

T. S. Eliot (1888–1965) was a well-known author, poet, and critic. After a long career setting out notable works, in 1948 he won the Nobel Prize for literature. The poems of his *Four Quartets* are interlinked meditations with the common theme of man's relationship with time, the universe, and the Divine. His understanding of the relationship between past and present and future show us a similarity in his thinking to that of Zecharia Sitchin.

Both men were raised in religious traditions. It is obvious that these men—both dedicated writers though in different disciplines—displayed similar perceptual and spiritual capabilities. Eliot developed an interest in native villages and the lifeways of early Native American peoples who lived before he was born, after seeing replicas of their villages at the 1904 World's Fair. We are reminded of Sitchin's early life growing up in Palestine where he was surrounded by evidence of the ancient lifeways of the peoples who lived on those same lands for centuries before him. Sitchin's work, mostly done just after Eliot's most productive period—in the early part of the twentieth century—delved deeply into the ancient scholarly evidence revealing ancient lifeways of the Nefilim. While these two men did not write about the same—or even similar—content, their mindsets and views of past, present, and future, obviously showed similar ways of thinking about time.

Sitchin did not have an early life filled with affluence as did Eliot. However, both were keen observers and penetrating thinkers. After rereading the translations of the first Sumerian scholars, Sitchin discovered a *different* story than that already published by scholars of the late nineteenth and early twentieth centuries. After close study of those early works, Sitchin wrote his own explanations, documenting them with translations from the ancient clay tablet sources to show the veracity of his reinterpretations. Eliot saw the same connectedness between past and present that characterized Sitchin's beliefs. With the exception that both men were creative and observant scholars, there their similarities end.

Sitchin showed inclinations to "hear different music" throughout his life. He was a man who did not just pass through life; he exercised his curiosity to fully understand its modern and ancient themes. Good old-fashioned diligent research work characterized

Sitchin's life as he followed his own inner guidance and pursued clues embedded in the ancient materials he studied throughout his life. This personal quality of persistence informed his lifelong "march to a different drummer."

In this book, we celebrate the published contributions made by Sitchin by selecting themes that emerged from his lifelong research into the ancient records. The now almost unknown *first* civilization he discovered, which was recorded in the ancient cuneiform, gave rise to what historians typically—and incorrectly—refer to as the Sumerian civilization. It became clear, as he unfolded his reinterpreted information, that a race of beings came *before* the Sumerians. Indeed, they were the "creators" of the human Sumerians. He studied the records with relish as they revealed the activities and lives of the Nefilim and Anunnaki— "those who came down."

As we have illustrated, what Sitchin learned from his study of the information scribed on what now are museum collections of clay tablets, was that the cuneiform script unfolded a different story than was promulgated by the early researchers. Sitchin's ability to think out of the box prompted him to reject earlier translations, and to unravel what had been unexplainable.

Sitchin gave the world a most valuable and important body of work and his lifelong effort to unravel the Sumerian sources is well deserving of accurate acknowledgment from everyone who is impressed by it. However, one disconcerting problem surfaces in many recent discussions. Far too many authors and self-defined experts seize on Sitchin-related content and *fail to attribute* their discussions to the actual source—Zecharia Sitchin. Whereas Sitchin's work was informed and guided by his close adherence to the actual tablet presentations, few—if any—of these secondhand writers are able to duplicate such skill, historical knowledge, and linguistic expertise. What they are doing, in essence, is piggybacking off his work. Because of the way the Internet allows unsubstantiated criticism to reach a wide audience, uninformed critics have taken shots at his work and seem to be getting away with this sort of plagiarism unscathed.

Academic (and popular) honesty and tradition demand that provocative and even mundane ideas be openly attributed to their original author. Failing to attribute any of Sitchin's research to him, before such borrowed (and in some cases stolen) information is brought to the public, especially in published form, is morally reprehensible. To omit attribution to Sitchin is a travesty because few can match his expertise and research diligence. Sitchin worked too long and hard to be ignored by any who would put his ideas, interpretations, and findings from his lifelong work into print with no mention of his unique and well-deserved contribution to Earth's ancient history. Enough said.

His notable contributions filled fourteen volumes of published materials in which he laid out considerable detail about the challenges faced by the Nibiru settlers who came to Earth. Sitchin found they bequeathed much more than just their presence to our ancient history. It is those themes of their accomplishments here on Earth, the love and strife that colored their lives, and their gifts of civilization—both good and bad features—that we highlight in this book.

It is important to understand that we have not attempted to rewrite Sitchin's work, but instead to craft an interpretation of his major findings, organized into seven chapters that serve to highlight what we believe are his most notable contributions. We have explored who the key players in that earthly civilization were, and the traditions developed on their home planet that they brought down. We looked into the practices, rules, and regulations that guided their behavior.

We also have explained the circumstances that prompted their chief scientist to undertake a genetically based experiment to solve a labor problem that threatened to disrupt their gold procurement mission. Using their advanced scientific knowledge, they *created humans* to become *willing workers*. Next we looked at an important personal proclivity of the Nefilim, their seeming preoccupation with love and lovemaking. It is entirely possible these behaviors were bequeathed to humans in the genes that they used to fashion humans in the creation process.

To refute what we believe to be the mistaken view that the advanced flying technology, now called UFOs (unidentified flying objects), regularly seen in the skies of the modern world could not have come from outer space, we have looked at Sitchin's evidence that flying objects have been seen in Earth's skies since ancient times, sent aloft from launch facilities whose remains *still are able to be seen* on Earth.

Then we explored a theme that seems to be pervasive in modern societies around the world—the use of *war* and warring tactics as a method to deal with territorial aggression and to resolve political disputes. When we delved into the origin of the idea of war, we found that it was a concept and set of practices that were *brought to Earth* by the Nefilim and Anunnaki. These space travelers taught the tactics and techniques of war and warring to humans who now have added to them. War's destructive methods and tools of annihilation now are rampant here on Earth, and hold dire warnings for our future existence.

Nuclear weapons were the most destructive of the technologies developed on the Anunnaki home planet and brought to Earth. Sitchin found in the tablet material that those devastating weapons first were used on Earth in 2024 BCE. Our final chapter focused on a topic Sitchin introduced at the end of his 2006 book, *The End of Days*. That topic is Armageddon—a term that has come to denote serious consequences for Earth's inhabitants. Sitchin points out that the coming of Armageddon is one of several prophecies he found in his research—the one he reports shifts prophecy from the realm of theology, eschatology, or mere historical curiosity to the matter of the very survival of humankind.

Sitchin held a strong belief that the information he found in the depths of ancient history holds important messages for our future. He points out that both the Hebrew Bible and the New Testament tell us that "the secrets of the Future are embedded in the Past." Sitchin explains that the destiny of Earth is connected to the Heavens, and that the affairs and fate of Mankind are linked to those of God and "gods." He repeatedly emphasized (in print and in his in-person presentations) that *history informs the future*. We have not identified *all* the many circumstances that Earth's population will face in the future that can be derived from the ancient records. However, Sitchin's discussions contain a number of clues we have teased out of his work to suggest future catastrophes.

We can draw on Sitchin's published discussions to identify some of the characteristics that prompted the Nefilim to show disdain for humans, and take action to address these issues. Although hundreds of years have passed since the Nefilim and Anunnaki left this planet, we can be reassured that Nibiru will return to Earth's vicinity after its approximate 3,600 Earth year orbit into and back from deep space, which will bring the Nefilim and Anunnaki back within reach of Earth. Several clues are given in Sitchin's work that should alert us to what our encounters with the Nefilim and Anunnaki may be like.

Given that intolerance seems to characterize the way earthlings treat all kinds of differences between and among Earth's peoples, we probably can expect humans to show a lack of acceptance (that is, fear and hostility aimed at destruction) of any beings who "come down." If the Nefilim act like this planet belongs to them (which in all likelihood, it does) nationalistic hostilities will be provoked. If they are perceived as invaders, earthlings may attempt to use weapons to repel these "other terrestrials"—but *with no success.*

We know that some UFO encounters have been treated with attacks by military planes. If that is the nature of our response to a Nefilim return, we can be assured that their weapons will overpower ours. We already have evidence that our weapons can be disabled by their technology. What we know from Sitchin's research is that the Nefilim and Anunnaki have very effective advanced weapons such as those that use beams that cause incapacitation and death to an enemy. In the event of a hostile encounter, humans will be eliminated by superior firepower until the Nefilim and Anunnaki achieve submission. The historical record Sitchin has provided supports this conclusion.

It is also likely the Nefilim will not be happy to see what humans have done to despoil this planet's life-giving resources. During the several hundreds of years of human existence after creation, when humans discovered that they had the ability to procreate, population growth ensued. In a relatively short time, it was out of control. Likely growth was exponential under Nefilim and Anunnaki rule, like it is in the modern world. Sitchin tells us that the tablets record the displeasure of the leader of the Earth mission (Enlil) who decried the hordes of people who lived on Earth, and their immoral behavior. At that time, he also saw that the population was gluttonous, and consuming the food supply. He allowed them to be washed away in what we know as Noah's Flood. That could happen again.

One very obvious reason for concern is that Earth has exceeded its *carrying capacity.** Scientists tell us that half of the world's population already does not have sufficient clean drinking water to support life. Insufficient food to feed Earth's teeming billions will be the next calamity. As in ancient times, several modern populations around the world are facing— currently or possibly in the near future—widespread starvation. The ice sheet on Antarctica now is unstable, and if dislodged, could bring another "great flood," annihilating much of Earth's population.†

Not only is population growth continuing, but civil unrest is spreading. Because of wars, despoliation of human habitats have generated migrations of large populations to areas that cannot provide food and water. Will the Nefilim help earthlings to resolve these problems, or will they just allow another global flood to reduce the size of the population? We pose such a ques-

---

*This is an ecological term that indicates that the amount of arable land capable of growing food is insufficient to supply the amount of food needed to adequately support the existing population.
†Scientists tell us that the interface between the Antarctic ice sheet and the underlying continent is becoming slushy and unstable. This would allow the ice sheet to be totally destabilized, as it was thirteen thousand years ago. If there are numerous tectonic events that produce another huge tsunami, such as the tectonic events predicted to accompany the return of Nibiru, a second global flood could be triggered.

tion for consideration. Only the unfolding future will be able to answer this question.

Will humankind rise to the challenges that Sitchin's work suggests to us? Or will the warnings in Sitchin's work be ignored? Humanity is facing a huge challenge. Not only are portions of the globe at war within national borders and with their neighbors over what could be called inconsequential issues (seen from a larger global and historical perspective), but some nations are striving to arm themselves for nuclear war. Perhaps there is a new "proverb" that characterizes humanity in these modern times: "Live in historical ignorance and die in nuclear flames."

One little man—Zecharia Sitchin—tried over several years to substitute facts for ignorance by providing information about the past that he believed informs the future. Was his life's work wasted? We shall see. The intent of this volume is to stimulate curious readers to study Sitchin's books for themselves. Sitchin offers many contributions in his fourteen volumes; a curious reader will be greatly rewarded for the effort required to read all of them.

If we sample just one of the thousands of Sitchin "fans" (former engineer, Lena Jacobson) for an assessment of the impact of Sitchin's contributions on her life, we see an insightful and thoughtful commentary:

Zecharia Sitchin changed my frame of reference, of both time and space. He elucidated a most crucial issue that has occupied my thoughts: what is the origin of planet Earth and its people? His body of work makes Sitchin a person of prophetic stature, a reincarnation of the biblical prophet Zecharia. The time came and that prophet was called to say what really happened in the past. And now, [in modern times], Zecharia Sitchin reveals what the stone stele and Sumerian clay tablets were silently telling us for several thousands of years. He made those artifacts speak in a poignant voice. Sitchin reported their story about the cradle of our civilization with such an authentic way that we experience all the thousands of years since Sumer in our own time.

In addition, like no other in the history of this planet, Sitchin positioned our planet in the Universe and showed its connection to other planets—and beyond. He let us know that we are not alone in the vast Universe, and thus he changed our time-space frame of reference. We learned from him the cosmic history of Earth, and thanks to his works, we now know what the Nefilim and Anunnaki told the Sumerians. We now know also to which "god" we owe our strengths and weaknesses. Most importantly, Zecharia Sitchin convincingly demythologized history. He changed both our view of the past and our perspectives for the future. For all these things I will be forever grateful to Zecharia Sitchin, who shared knowledge about the connection of Heaven and Earth. This makes him not only a prophet, but the *greatest historian of our time*.[1]

We are facing a most interesting and challenging future. Sitchin's information will suggest some things we can do to prepare for it. Let's vow to take his work seriously and make the effort needed to move forward and build an informed future. As the character who made space exploration a most exciting and popular future—Captain Jean-Luc Picard of the Starship *Enterprise*—tells us: "Make it so!"

Appendix A

Understanding Nuclear Weapons

Developing a nuclear weapon is not an easy task. It involves a complex set of processes that require specialized manpower, materials, and equipment. It also is a multimillion dollar endeavor that takes years to complete. However, understanding what these processes involve is useful in order to knowledgeably interpret information regarding a nation's attempts to join the world's "nuclear elite." Here we will present a layman's explanation that will allow the interested reader to become oriented to and conversant with the terminology and the several steps in the process.

It must be pointed out that since 1946 when the first modern era detonations on two cities in the country of Japan brought nuclear weapons to the forefront of public concern, several professional organizations have been developed to carry out the United Nations' restrictions (and world's concerns) to limit proliferation of these weapons. These organizations are the Carnegie Endowment for International Peace with physicist James Acton, the International Atomic Energy Association (IAEA), and the World Nuclear Association.

Developing a Nuclear Weapon

Our source for this discussion is a BBC Futures report by writer Geoff Brumfiel from November 18, 2014. Brumfiel's article, "Become a Nuclear Superpower . . . in Ten Steps," explains the process used for nuclear development (available at www.bbc.com/ future/story/20120607-nuclear-weapons-in-ten-steps).

The process begins with obtaining the necessary isotope uranium-235. The most abundant isotope in nature is uranium-238, which will not sustain nuclear reactions. Only a very small percentage of naturally occurring uranium is U-235. It is possible to transform uranium-238 into U-235 using a complex process of refinement. Experts report that even the simplest weapon requires about 50 kilograms of 90 percent pure uranium U-235. The development process requires considerable testing and repetition called "redundancy," so the actual amount of U-235 needed is 330 pounds, or around twenty tons of U-238.

The isotope U-238, known as "yellowcake," is obtained by purchasing it or (as in the case of Iran) mining it. The world's biggest supplier of U-238 is the company known as Kazatomprom, Kazakhstan's nationalized nuclear power company. Upon obtaining it, storage is the next challenge, one that requires a nuclear facility.* This raw material must be refined to *convert* it into U-235, the fissionable substance. Therein lies the larger challenge.

The manpower needed to undertake this processing work consists of scientists, engineers, and technicians. Most important, properly trained experts do not come cheap. Such a qualified team must have extensive knowledge of nuclear chemistry,

---

*Iran stores its supply of yellowcake at a facility in Isfahan located south of Tehran.

nuclear physics, and several related disciplines. They must know the behavior of isotopes at various stages of the processes involved.

These experts will know that nuclear processes work on a simple principle: when a heavy nucleus of an atom splits, it converts a tiny amount of mass into pure energy. Their expertise is particularly important because serious dangers are faced when a chain reaction gets out of hand. Nuclear blasts are triggered through an uncontrolled chain reaction in a large block of material, where each new split causes more splits, releasing more energy. However, most radioactive materials will not sustain a chain reaction. Energy produced in the nuclear development process has many uses other than weapons development, such as to treat cancer or generate electricity.

U-238 is three neutrons heavier than U-235. To get yellowcake into a more useful gaseous form, a team of researchers must follow a simple recipe: heat it to burn off impurities, then expose it to hydrogen fluoride to make an intermediate product, uranium tetrafluoride. This process must be done in a kiln filled with fluorine gas. If the process is successful, gaseous uranium hexafluoride results. This last is dangerous because the chemical is corrosive and must be handled very carefully.

Then a powerful centrifuge that spins at tens of thousands of rotations per minute is needed to *separate the U-235 from the U-238*. These substances are in very small atomic masses and it is very difficult to separate the heaver form to obtain the lighter ones. The expert who performed the supply role for the Pakistani nuclear bomb in 2004 (Abdul Qadeer Khan according to the BBC source) indicated that he also supplied centrifuge designs, parts, and expertise to Iran, North Korea, and Libya. (Libya's ability to collect all the technology needed to get their process to completion proved impossible. They abandoned their efforts.)

The words of our source, Geoff Brumfiel, are essential here to authentically convey Iran's progress in working through these processes to acquire the necessary amount of enriched weapons-grade U-235:

> Regardless of how they do it, a country will need *several thousand centrifuges*. These must be strung together into "cascades" that can enrich the uranium hexafluoride gas made earlier. By passing the uranium hexafluoride from cascade to cascade, uranium-235 begins to slowly accumulate. *Iran has been working on enrichment since the early 2000s and in February 2010 said it had begun processing uranium to 20% enrichment*. This has civilian uses but also *is a significant step towards producing weapons-grade uranium* (emphases added).[1]

Important to our main discussion of the threat posed by Iran's nuclear development program is the next step. Experts say that if a state is careful in its use of its centrifuges, it can accumulate enough uranium-235 for a bomb in less than a year. To obtain the needed 330 pounds for two or three bombs to be made would take less than two years.

The delivery system to get the uranium to its target is a vital step. There is more than one method of delivering the "payload," but each has its drawbacks and advantages. The IAEA (the international inspection/oversight agency) indicates from their intelligence and inspection experience that Iran is working on an "implosion" delivery system for the bomb they are designing. This style of weapon works by packing explosives around a package of U-235 (held inside a sphere) that, when detonated, would squeeze the package until it reaches critical mass. This type of weapon requires a hard-to-design neutron detonator that will give the weapon its "jolt" at just the right time. The advantages of this complex implosion device are that it requires less U-235 and it *can fit on top of a missile.*

The next step is to get the uranium out of gaseous form and into a metallic state. A simple recipe using water, hydrofluoric acid, and magnesium makes this transformation possible. With the metal ready, it has to be machined into the desired shape: either two halves of a sphere for an implosion weapon, or discs for a gun-type device.*

The final step is to *test* the bomb and its delivery system. This is where the world's attention is brought to focus on the nation that has undertaken this process. With all the intelligence and oversight structures, any nation working on nuclear development will not be out of the world's attention for very long. The testing stage likely will prompt a punitive reaction from the world community with the leveling of serious sanctions.

The benefits of getting to the testing stage is that it signals to the world that the nation under study is "ready." The population of the nation that is successful in achieving nuclear weapons benefits with an increase in pride of their nation's accomplishment. The world then shines a spotlight on that country, after all the thwarting efforts aimed at the ambitious country, no nation can win. Having said that, having a ready system means the source of a strike can be known, but "when it will happen" still is unknown.

---

*We have omitted the description of the "gun type" delivery system as that is not the one that Iran is developing.

The Case of the Evil Wind

By Zecharia Sitchin

In this article, which was originally posted on Sitchin's personal website in November 2001, Sitchin presents the case that the ancient phenomena that appeared to more recent scientists to be due to climate change was instead the aftermath of a nuclear explosion that occurred in 2024 BCE. He refers to that event as generating an "evil wind." The article is available at www.sitchin.com/evilwind.htm.

THE CASE OF THE EVIL WIND

Climate Study Corroborates Sumer's Nuclear Fate

© Z. Sitchin. Reprinted with Permission

At the end of the third millennium B.C. the great Sumerian civilization came to an abrupt end. Its sudden demise was bewailed in numerous lamentation texts that have been discovered by archeologists. The texts ascribed the calamity to an "Evil Wind" that came blowing from the west (from the direction of the Mediterranean Sea)—a deathly cloud that caused excruciating death to all living beings, people and animals alike, that withered plants and poisoned the waters.

In *The Wars of Gods and Men* (third book of The Earth Chronicles series), Zecharia Sitchin saw an explanation of the sudden death in a long text known to scholars as the *Erra Epos,* that described a chain of events that ultimately led to the use of "Weapons of Terror" in a conflict between opposing clans of the Anunnaki ("Those who from Heaven to Earth came").

Based on the descriptions of the weapons in the Erra Epos and in the lamentation texts, Zecharia Sitchin concluded that the Weapons of Terror were *nuclear weapons.* Used to obliterate the spaceport that then existed in the Sinai Peninsula (and some "sinning cities" such as Sodom and Gomorrah), the nuclear cloud then was carried by the prevailing winds eastward, causing death and desolation in the Lands Between the Rivers (Mesopotamia)—the empire of Sumer and Akkad.

Besides claiming that nuclear weapons were first used on Earth not in the 1940s in Hiroshima, but thousands of years earlier in the Near East, Zecharia also pinpointed the date: 2024 B.C.!

Scientific Corroboration Now Comes Along

That the civilization that sprang out in Sumer circa 3800 B.C.—reaching unparalleled heights under the last dynasty, the Third Dynasty of Ur (Abraham's city)—had come to an abrupt end near the end of the third millennium B.C. has been an accepted and well documented fact. That the end was abrupt, was also certain. What scholars deemed as still lacking was an explanation: How, what caused it?

Beginning in 1999, archaeologists and scholars specializing in the Near East saw mounting evidence that the demise of Sumer and Akkad (Sumer's northern extension) coincided with an abrupt climate change. An initial study by Harvey Weiss and Timothy C. Weiskel of Harvard University was reinforced by a subsequent study (*Geology*, April 2000) by H. M. Cullen et. al. from the Lamont-Doherty Earth Observatory of Columbia University, the University of Utah, the Lawrence Livermore National Laboratory, and the Institute fur Geowissenschaften, Germany. Based on studies of unexplained aridity and wind-blown dust storms and radiocarbon datings, they reported that their readings indicated a date of 4025 years ago (plus or minus a margin of 125 years).

A Precise Date Corroborated!

Those and similar climate-change studies, relating the climate conditions to the rise and fall of civilizations in the Old as well as the New Worlds, were summed up in a major study published in the prestigious journal *Science* in its 27 April 2001 issue. Authored by Peter B. deMenocal of the Lamont-Doherty Earth Observatory of Columbia University, the study paid particular attention to sedimentary remains of Tephra; the telltale rock fragments confirmed the date 4025 Years Before Present.

And 4025 years, before the present year, A.D. 2001—is exactly 2024 B.C., as Zecharia Sitchin had determined in his 1985 book!

The Tephra Mystery

The reliance of this latest study on the Tephra evidence is doubly significant.

While the previous studies spoke of "wind blown dust," this latest study focuses on the material called *Tephra*. And what is Tephra? It is defined in geology textbooks thus:

> When a volcano erupts, it will sometimes eject material such as rock fragments into the atmosphere. This material is known as *Tephra*

These burnt-through pieces of blackened gravel-like rock mostly fall near their volcanic source; but ashlike particles can be carried by prevailing winds over many miles and can stay aloft for more than a year.

The area in the Sinai Peninsula where the destroyed spaceport had been is indeed covered—to this day!—with gravelike [sic] burnt-through blackened stones (for photo evidence see illustrations 105, 106, and 107 in *The Wars of Gods and Men*). But as Zecharia has pointed out in his book; there are NO VOLCANOES in the Sinai Peninsula. In the Sinai Peninsula, the source of the wind-carried dust remains a mystery.

And the only explanation for these broken and blackened stones in the Sinai and the windblown desolation in Mesopotamia can be the tale of the *Erra Epos*, (reflected in the biblical tale of the upheaval of Sodom and Gomorrah): not an eruption by a non-existent volcano, but the use of nuclear weapons in 2024 B.C.

ZS / November 2001

Notes

Note to Readers: Page references in Zecharia Sitchin's works are to the hardcover editions published by Bear & Company.

Prologue.
Zecharia Sitchin—Author, Ancient Historian, and Explorer of Archaeology

1. Human Potential Foundation, *When Cosmic Cultures Meet,* 164.
2. Ibid, 164.
3. Ibid., 166.

Introduction. Sitchin's Space-Age Paradigm

1. Evans, *Legacy of Zecharia Sitchin,* 80.
2. Sitchin, *The Wars of Gods and Men,* 75–76.
3. Ibid., 76
4. Sitchin, *The 12th Planet,* 292–4.
5. Kramer, *From the Tablets of Sumer.*
6. Sitchin, *The 12th Planet,* 303.
7. Sitchin, *The 12th Planet,* viii.
8. Ibid., 13.

Chapter 1.
The Astronauts from Outer Space

1. Sitchin, *The 12th Planet,* 131.
2. Ibid., 264.
3. Ibid., 260.

4. Sitchin, *The Wars of Gods and Men,* 85.

5. Sitchin, *The 12th Planet,* 56.

Chapter 2.
The Anunnaki Family Tree

1. Sitchin, *The 12th Planet,* 88.

2. Ibid., 56.

3. Ibid., 88.

4. Ibid., 119.

5. Sitchin, *The Wars of Gods and Men,* 85.

6. Sitchin, *The 12th Planet,* 90.

7. Falkenstein, *Sumerische Goetterlieder,* vol. VII.

8. Sitchin, *The Wars of Gods and Men,* 193.

9. Sitchin, *The Wars of Gods and Men,* 345–350.

10. Ibid., 194.

11. Kramer, *History Begins at Sumer.*

12. Sitchin, *The 12th Planet,* 100.

13. Ibid., 261.

14. Ibid.

15. Ibid., 336.

16. Ibid., 354.

17. Ibid., 355.

18. Sitchin, *The Wars of Gods and Men,* 119.

19. Sitchin, *The 12th Planet,* 93.

20. Ibid.

21. Sitchin, *The Wars of Gods and Men,* 95.

22. Sitchin, *The 12th Planet,* 96.

23. Ibid., 310.

24. Ibid., 311.

25. Ibid., 354.

26. Sitchin, *The Wars of Gods and Men,* 167.

27. Ibid., 117.

28. Sitchin, *The End of Days,* 53.

29. Sitchin, *The Wars of Gods and Men,* 226.

30. Ibid., 227.

31. Farrell, *The Giza Death Star,* 42–47.

32. Sitchin, *The 12th Planet,* 102.

33. Ibid., 102–106.

34. Ibid., 106.
35. Ibid., 193.
36. Ibid., 303.
37. Ibid., 349–356.

Chapter 3. The Creation of Earthlings

1. Sitchin, *The 12th Planet,* 301.
2. Ibid., 303.
3. Ibid.
4. Sitchin, *Divine Encounters,* 44–47.
5. Sitchin, *The 12th Planet,* 304.
6. Ibid., 302.
7. Ibid.
8. Ibid.
9. Ibid., 305.
10. Human Potential Foundation, *When Cosmic Cultures Meet,* 163–167.
11. Sitchin, *The 12th Planet,* 308.
12. Ibid., 305.
13. Sitchin, *The Wars of Gods and Men,* 106.
14. Sitchin, *The 12th Planet,* 302.
15. Ibid., 318.
16. Ibid.
17. Ibid., 317.
18. Ibid., 325.
19. Ibid., 326.
20. Ibid., 328.
21. Ibid., 303.

Chapter 4. Anunnaki Love and Lovemaking

1. Sitchin, *The 12th Planet,* 335–36.
2. Ibid., 161.
3. Sitchin, *The Stairway to Heaven,* 119.
4. Sitchin, *Divine Encounters,* 167.
5. Ibid.
6. Ibid., 16.
7. Sitchin, *The 12th Planet,* 94.
8. Ibid., 94.
9. Ibid., 95.

10. Ibid.

11. Ibid., 101–102.

12. Ibid., 101.

13. Sitchin, *The Wars of Gods and Men,* 82.

14. Ibid.

15. Ibid., 216.

16. Ibid., 82.

17. Ibid., 153.

18. Ibid., 216.

19. Ibid., 217.

20. Ibid., 219–220.

21. Sitchin, *The Stairway to Heaven,* 119.

22. Ibid.

23. Sitchin, *Divine Encounters,* 168.

24. Sitchin, *The Wars of Gods and Men,* 239.

25. Ibid., 240.

26. Ibid.

27. Ibid.

28. Ibid.

29. Sitchin, *Divine Encounters,* 170.

30. Sitchin, *Divine Encounters,* 172.

31. Ibid.

32. Sitchin, *There Were Giants Upon the Earth,* 266.

33. Ibid., 267.

34. Ibid., 269.

35. Sitchin, *Divine Encounters,* 73.

Chapter 5. Wonderful Flying Machines

1. Sitchin, *The Wars of Gods and Men,* 95.

2. Ibid., 83.

3. Sitchin, *The 12th Planet,* 122.

4. Ibid.

5. Ibid., 123.

6. Ibid., 134.

7. Ibid., 124–28.

8. Sitchin, *The Wars of Gods and Men,* 236.

9. Ibid., 237.

10. Sitchin, *The 12th Planet,* 134–35.

11. Sitchin, *The Wars of Gods and Men,* 123.
12. Sitchin, *When Time Began,* 148.
13. Ibid., 165–66.
14. Sitchin, *The Wars of Gods and Men,* 118.
15. Ibid., 70.
16. Ibid., 93.
17. Huneeus "Exploring the Anunnaki-UFO Link."
18. Rubstov, Mutual UFO Network 1994 Symposium Proceedings.
19. UFO Sightings Daily, "Many UFO Sightings Over Mecklenburg Nuclear Power Plant, May 2014, UFO Sighting News," www.ufosightingsdaily .com/2014/05/many-ufo-sightings-over-mecklenburg.html.
20. George D. Fawcett, "UFOs Continue to Visit Nuclear Energy Sites," www.rense.com/general20/fo.htm.
21. Dream Prophecy blog, "UFOs Over Chernobyl and Fukushima Nuclear Power Plants," http://dream-prophecy.blogspot.com/2013/07/ufos-over-chernobyl-and-fukushima.html
22. Barracuda Smith, "Giant UFO Hovering Over Fukushima Nuclear Power Plant, April 12," online video, www.dailymotion.com/video/ xi89jc_giant-ufo-hovering-over-fukushima-nuclear-plant-april12_news.

Chapter 6.
War and Warring—An Earthly Inclination?

1. Cohen, a review of "A History of Warfare," by John Keegan.
2. Smith, *The Most Dangerous Animal.*
3. Sitchin, *The Wars of Gods and Men,* 83.
4. Ibid., 91.
5. Ibid., 95.
6. Ibid., 91.
7. Ibid., 92.
8. Ibid., 99.
9. Ibid., 28.
10. Ibid., 29.
11. Ibid., 31.
12. Ibid.
13. Ibid., 155.
14. Ibid., 162.
15. Ibid.
16. Ibid.

17. Ibid.
18. Ibid.

Chapter 7. Armageddon—Global Catastrophe?

1. *Watchtower,* May 15, 1990
2. Jerold Aust, "Armageddon—The Last Day of the World?" at www.ucg
   .org/the-good-news/armageddon-the-end-of-the-world.
3. "Armageddon," *Wikipedia,* http://en.wikipedia.org/wiki/Armageddon.
4. Sitchin, *The Wars of Gods and Men,* 1.
5. Ibid.
6. Sitchin, *The End of Days,* 2.
7. Sitchin, *The Wars of Gods and Men,* 131.
8. Ibid., 304.
9. Ibid., 305.
10. Ibid.
11. Ibid., 306.
12. Ibid., 325.
13. Ibid., 326.
14. Ibid.
15. Ibid., 328–9.
16. Ibid., 329.
17. Sitchin, *There Were Giants Upon the Earth,* 289.
18. "Libya and Weapons of Mass Destruction," *Wikipedia,* https://
    en.wikipedia.org/wiki/Libya_and_weapons_of_mass_destruction
19. Ryan Mauro, "Understanding Islamic Extremism," The Clarion Project,
    www.clarionproject.org/section/understanding-radical-islam.
20. Henchy, "Building a framework," 1–9.

Epilogue. The Past Informs the Future

1. Evans, *The Legacy of Zecharia Sitchin,* 115.

Appendix A. Understanding Nuclear Weapons

1. Geoff Brumfiel, "Become a Nuclear Superpower—In 10 Steps," *BBC,*
   November 18, 2014, www.bbc.com/future/story/20120607-nuclear-
   weapons-in-ten-steps.

Bibliography

Alford, Alan F. *Gods of the New Millennium.* Walsall, UK: Eridu Books, 1996.

Blamires, Steve. *The Irish Celtic Magic Tradition.* London: Aquarian Press, 1992.

Budge, E. A. *The Gods of the Egyptians.* New York: Dover Books, 1969.

Cohen, Eliot. Review of *A History of Warfare,* by John Eliot. *Columbia/ SPICA,* March/April 1994.

Cornish, Edward. "Toward a Philosophy of Futurism." *The Futurist* II (6): 360–361.

Cremo, Michael A. and Richard L. Thompson. *Forbidden Archeology: The Hidden History of the Human Race.* Los Angeles, Calif.: Bhaktivedanta Book Publishing, Inc., 1993.

Darwin, Charles. *On the Origin of Species by Means of Natural Selection, or the Preservation of Favoured Races in the Struggle for Life.* London: John Murray, 1859.

Delaport, Louis. *Mesopotamia.* London: Kegan Paul, Trench, Trubner & Co., 1925.

DeMarco, Frank. *The Cosmic Internet: Explanations From the Other Side.* Faber, Va.: Rainbow Ridge Books, 2011.

Ebstein, R. P. "The Molecular Genetic Architecture of Human Personality: Beyond Self-report Questionnaires." *Molecular Psychiatry* 11 (2006): 427–445.

Evans, M. J. *The Legacy of Zecharia Sitchin.* San Diego, Calif.: The Book Tree, 2011.

———. "The Paradigm Has Shifted: What's Next?" in *Of Heaven and Earth:*

Essays Presented at the First Sitchin Studies Day, edited by Zecharia Sitchen. Escondido, Calif.: The Book Tree, 1996.

Falkenstein, Adam. *Sumerische Goetterlieder,* 1959.

Farrell, Joseph P. *The Giza Death Star Deployed: The Physics and Engineering of the Great Pyramid.* Kempton, Ill.: Adventures Unlimited, 2003.

Finch, Robert and Cordell Svenglis. *Futures Unlimited: Teaching About Worlds to Come.* Washington D.C.: National Council for the Social Studies, 1979.

Freer, Neil. *Breaking the Godspell: The Politics of Our Evolution.* Escondido, Calif.: The Book Tree, 2000.

Henchey, Norman. "Building a Framework for the Study of the Future," *World Future Society Bulletin* XI (5), September–October, 1–9, 1977.

Human Potential Foundation. *When Cosmic Cultures Meet: An International Conference Presented by the Human Potential Foundation.* Falls Church, Va.: Human Potential Foundation, 1995.

Huneeus, Antonio. "Exploring the Anunnaki—UFO Link," in *Of Heaven and Earth: Essays Presented at the First Sitchin Studies Day.* Escondido, Calif.: The Book Tree, 1996.

Kean, Leslie. "Symington Confirms He Saw UFO 10 Years Ago," *Daily Courier,* March 18, 2007.

King, Leonard W. *Babylonian Magic and Sorcery.* London: Kessinger, 1896.

———. *The Seven Tablets of Creation, or the Babylonian and Assyrian Legends Concerning the Creation of the World and of Mankind.* London: Luzac and Company, 1902.

Kramer, Samuel N. *History Begins at Sumer.* New York: Doubleday and Company, 1959.

———. *The Sumerians: Their History, Culture, and Character.* Chicago: Chicago University Press, 1963.

Kuhn, Thomas S. "Resistance by Scientists to Scientific Discovery," *Science* CXXXIV, 596–602, 1961.

———. *The Structure of Scientific Revolutions.* 2nd ed., enlarged. Chicago: The University of Chicago Press, 1970.

Langdon, Stephen. *Sumerian and Babylonian Psalms.* New York: P. Geuthner, G. E. Stechert & Company, 1909.

Langdon, Stephen. *The Epic of Gilgamesh. Publications of the Babylonian Section,* Vol. 10, no. 3. Philadelphia: University of Philadelphia Museum, 1917.

Layard, A. H. *Nineveh and Its Remains.* London: John Murray, 1849.

Layard, A, H. *Inscriptions in the Cuneiform Character from Assyrian Monuments.* London: Harrison and Sons, 1851.

Mackenzie, Donald. *Mythology of the Babylonian People.* London: Bracken Books, 1915.

O'Brien, Christian, with Barbara J. O'Brien. *Genius of the Few.* Rev. ed. Bristol, UK: Dianthus Publishing, 1999.

Petersen, John L. *Out of the Blue: How to Anticipate Wild Cards and Big Future Surprises.* Washington D.C.: The Arlington Institute, 1997.

———. *The Road to 2015: Profiles of the Future.* N.p.: Waite Group Press, 1994.

———. *A Vision for 2012: Planning for Extraordinary Change.* Golden, Colo.: Fulcrum Publishers, 2008.

Rawlingson, Henry C. *The Cuneiform Inscrptions of Western Asia.* London: The British Museum, 1861.

Sitchin, Zecharia. *The Cosmic Code: Book VI of the Earth Chronicles.* Rochester, Vt.: Bear & Company, 2002. First published in 1998 by Avon Books.

———. *Divine Encounters: A Guide to Visions, Angels and Other Emissaries.* Rochester, Vt.: Bear & Company, 2002. First published in 1995 by Avon Books.

———. *The Earth Chronicles Expedition.* Rochester, Vt.: Bear & Company, 2007.

———. *The Earth Chronicles Handbook: A Comprehensive Guide to the Seven Books of the Earth Chronicles.* Rochester, Vt.: Bear & Company, 2009.

———. *The End of Days: Armageddon and Prophecies of the Return: The 7th and Concluding Book of the Earth Chronicles.* Rochester, Vt.: Bear & Company, 2014. First published in 2007 by William Morrow.

———. *Genesis Revisited: Is Modern Science Catching Up with Ancient Knowledge?* Rochester, Vt.: Bear & Company, 2002. First published in 1990 by Avon Books.

———. *Journeys to the Mythical Past.* Rochester, Vt.: Bear & Company, 2007.

———. *The King Who Refused to Die.* Rochester, Vt.: Bear & Company, 2012.

———. *The Lost Book of Enki: Memoirs and Prophecies of an Extraterrestrial God.* Rochester, Vt.: Bear & Company, 2001.

———. *The Lost Realms: Book IV of the Earth Chronicles.* Rochester, Vt.: Bear & Company, 1990. First published in 1990 by Avon Books.

————, ed. *Of Heaven and Earth: Essays Presented at the First Sitchin Studies Day.* Escondido, Calif.: The Book Tree, 1996.

————. *The Stairway to Heaven: Book II of the Earth Chronicles.* Rochester, Vt.: Bear & Company, 1992. First published in 1980 by St. Martin's Press.

————. *There Were Giants Upon the Earth: Gods, Demigods, and Human Ancestry: The Evidence of Alien DNA.* Rochester, Vt.: Bear & Company, 2010.

————. *The 12th Planet: Book I of the Earth Chronicles.* Rochester, Vt.: Bear & Company, 1991. First published in 1976 by Stein and Day.

————. *The Wars of Gods and Men: Book III of the Earth Chronicles.* Rochester, Vt.: Bear & Company, 1992. First published in 1985 by Avon Books.

————. *When Time Began: Book V of the Earth Chronicles.* Rochester, Vt.: Bear & Company, 1994. First published in 1993 by Avon Books.

Smith, David Livingston. *The Most Dangerous Animal: Human Nature and the Origins of War.* New York: St. Martin's Griffin, 2009.

Smith, George. *The Chaldean Accounts of Genesis: From the Cuneiform Inscriptions.* London: Marston, Searle & Rivington, 1980.

Tellinger, Michael. *African Temples of the Anunnaki: The Lost Technologies of the Gold Mines of Enki.* Rochester, Vt.: Inner Traditions/Bear & Company, 2013.

Von Rad, Gerhard. *Genesis.* London: SCM Press, 1961.

Index

Page numbers in *italics* indicate illustrations.

About the Author

M. J. Evans, Ph.D., is professor emeritus at the State University of New York's Empire State College (ESC). She is a graduate of Utica College of Syracuse University (BA 1966, *cum laude*) and Syracuse University's Maxwell School (M.A. and Ph.D., 1979). She taught for thirty years as a member of the full-time faculty at ESC. Her disciplinary expertise focuses on physical and cultural geography, map perception, environmental studies, future studies, ancient landscapes, and global environmental issues. She retired in 2004 and was awarded the honorary title of Professor Emeritus. She now focuses on travel, research, and writing.

In 1990 Evans began to examine the landscapes lived on by ancient peoples. She accompanied Zecharia Sitchin on tours to ancient sites and landscapes in Greece; England; Israel; the islands of Malta, Santorini, and Crete; as well as the Yucatán of Mexico. Her personal travels took her to ancient sites in England, Wales, Scotland, Ireland, southern France, Israel, and Turkey. She gave particular attention to the landscapes used by ancient peoples for their settlements and the huge megastone structures they often built.

She was invited by Sitchin to be one of six presenters at the first "Sitchin Studies Day" in 1996. She authored a chapter for that conference's proceedings (*Of Heaven and Earth: Essays Presented at the First Sitchin Studies Day*) titled "The Paradigm Has Shifted—Now What?" Thereafter she published a work titled *The Legacy of Zecharia Sitchin* (The Book Tree, 2011) where she argued that his scholarly work indeed has shifted the explanatory paradigm on human origins. She believes that his evidence clearly documents that an ancient civilization developed on planet Earth 445,000 years ago and genetically created modern humans.

Evans has appeared on four nationally televised programs in the "Ancient Aliens" series (Prometheus Productions) explaining Sitchin's work. She also is a regular reviewer of new publications dealing with global issues for the American Library Association's CHOICE, a publication used by academic librarians to choose additions to their university's collection.

M. J. Evans now studies geographic landscapes and ancient sites in Turkey, where she lives for most of each year. Her United States residence is in the mountains of North Carolina.